THE LIFE OF A BOY BORN IN INDONESIA

THE LIFE OF A BOY BORN IN INDONESIA

by
RENÉ LEIDELMEYER

INKWATER PRESS
PORTLAND · OREGON
INKWATERPRESS.COM

Copyright © 2020 by Pierre René Leidelmeyer

Edited by Linda Franklin
Cover and interior design by Masha Shubin

Beautiful Sunrise Over The Jatiluwih Rice Terraces in Bali © Tarch. BigStockPhoto.com

All rights reserved. No part of this book may be reproduced or transmitted in any form or by any means whatsoever, including photocopying, recording or by any information storage and retrieval system, without written permission from the publisher and/or author. The views and opinions expressed in this book are those of the author(s) and do not necessarily reflect those of the publisher, and the publisher hereby disclaims any responsibility for them. Neither is the publisher responsible for the content or accuracy of the information provided in this document. Contact Inkwater Press at inkwater.com. 503.968.6777

Publisher: Inkwater Press | www.inkwaterpress.com

ISBN-13 978-1-62901-668-9 | ISBN-10 1-62901-668-3

1 3 5 7 9 10 8 6 4 2

CONTENTS

Java 1
Time in School 3
Learning How to Fish 5
Getting Accepted by the (Dessa) Village People 10
Things I Did and Learned from My Native Friends .. 16
The Excitement of Kite Combat 44
The Japanese Occupation (1942–1945) 72
Entertainment the Natives Enjoyed 95
The Indonesian Revolution (1945–1947) 110
Moving into the Women's Camp 138
Freedom at Last 143
Work Experiences 164
Home Again 196
What is an INDO? 226
About the Author 227

JAVA

I WAS BORN ON THE island of Java in 1930. There were seven in the family, my parents and five kids. I had an older brother, an older sister, and two younger brothers. My father worked for the railroads. My parents liked to have parties and played cards on Friday nights. We lived in a big house with servants' quarters.

My parents were both of mixed European and Indonesian heritage, which made us Indos – neither Europeans nor natives, but an intermediate group. We had seven servants. Some of the servants lived in the servants' quarters and some went home each night. We had two for in the house, one who did all the cleaning, and one who mainly served us during breakfast, lunch and dinner and when there was company. She also made sure that the horse-drawn carriage was on time to take us to school and back. We had one servant to prepare our meals. She was a very good cook and she oversaw the servants. Another servant did the laundry and ironing. There was no washing machine, so she did the laundry on a washboard at the well. She dried the clothes on the wash lines in the sun and kept her iron hot with wood coals that she had to fan constantly. It would take her all day to do the laundry for our family of seven. Another servant would take care of us five kids. She had a busy schedule. She had to make sure that we stayed in our rooms from 2:00 to 4:00 p.m. because at that time of the day it was too hot to be in the sun. At night and in the morning, she had to go through our rooms and make sure there were no mosquitoes under the netting around our beds.

We also had a young man who took care of the animals. We had chickens, ducks, pigeons, sheep, goats, guinea pigs, rabbits, and all sorts of birds. His day would start before sunrise. He had to clean the birdcages and the stalls. Then he had to find grass for the sheep, guinea pigs and rabbits. He also cut brush for the goats. Sometimes during the dry season my mother would buy brush and grass from kids out of the dessa (village).

In my opinion there were three classes of native Indonesians. First, there were the rich and well educated who owned businesses and had servants. Second, there were those who worked in factories, hotels, stores, drove taxis or were servants. Last were the ones who lived in the villages. The villagers were often street vendors who brought their goods such as fruits and vegetables, chickens, etc., to the market. Early in the morning they walked along the road to get to the market. The women walked with heavy baskets on their heads and a child on their back. The men would wear a yoke over their shoulders to carry two heavy baskets full of merchandise. They walked for hours to get to the market. In the evening they returned home with a lighter load. Many of these people did not know how to read or write and did not know their own age. Although they were less educated they were very good at managing money. This group of people became my friends.

TIME IN SCHOOL

MY SIBLINGS AND I went to Catholic school. During first to third grade we went to school from 7:30 to 11:30 a.m. When we entered fourth grade we went to school until 1:00 p.m. This schedule continued through seventh grade. I always looked forward to the ride to school because I always sat next to the driver of the horse-drawn carriage. The school was divided in half by an eight-foot-high chain-link fence. On one side of the fence all the lessons were taught in Dutch, and on the other side the lessons were taught in both Indonesian and Dutch. I went to the Dutch school. There were many school and church activities but the two schools never attended events together.

At home in the afternoon and evening we did many activities like sports coached by some of the parents in the neighborhood, and played games and music. I played soccer and badminton. Every day after dinner from 5:00 in the afternoon until 7:00 p.m. we had free time. After that we had homework time and if we did not have any, my father gave us some. We had to keep our grades up in school because anything less than an A was considered failing by my father. I had a hard time in school because I was often sick with malaria. The medicine I had to take for it, quinine powder, tasted awful. It was so bitter when I swallowed it that I felt like my eardrums were popping out. When I had a malaria attack, I had to take the medicine three times a day and then it felt like I had bees buzzing in my head. Many days I had to catch up on schoolwork when the other kids were playing sports and doing other activities. Since I missed out on time with the other kids, I spent a lot of time with my animals.

LEARNING HOW TO FISH

MY NEIGHBOR FRIENDS, BOYS my age, came over to my house to show me fish they caught. I was very impressed and wanted to know where and how they did it. They told me that they went fishing with their father and a guide in the ocean. They showed me the fishing equipment they used, all heavy and expensive gear designed for saltwater fishing. When my father came home from work, I told him the fish story and asked him if he would take me fishing someday. My father was not interested; he said if I wanted fish, he would take me to the fish market. I was disappointed. I told the fish story to my houseboy, whom I called Sam. Sam said if I wanted to fish, he would teach me. I jumped on the offer and told Sam that I would ask my father to buy the fishing gear, but Sam said he would make our fishing gear.

The next day when I came home from school Sam showed me the fishing poles he made. The poles were made from bamboo and they were so thin that I thought they could never hold any fish. Sam told me to go to my father to ask for an old guitar string. Sam made fish hooks out of the old guitar string, very tiny hooks with a barb and everything. Then Sam told me to go to the neighbor down the street who had horses to ask him for the long horsehairs from the tail. My neighbor wanted to know what the horsehair was for. I told him Sam was making fishing line from it, and the neighbor said that he would like to see the end product. Sam made several six- to ten-foot thin strands without any knots. I took them over to the neighbor and showed him. The neighbor said that it was very clever and if I needed more horsehair to just get it. Now I was ready to go fishing but Sam said that the rice plants had to be a certain height. I did not know what the height of the rice plants had to do with it. I was confused and dropped the subject. Sam said that he would let me know when it was time.

After what felt like a long time, one day after school Sam said we would go fishing tomorrow. First, we had to get some bait, so he took me to the manure pile, and we started digging. There were many worms in the pile. Sam told me to pick up the worms, but to leave the big ones. In my mind it was his job, but then Sam said, "If you don't pick up the worms you can't catch any fish." The next morning at 6:00 a.m. when I went to the servants' quarters everything was ready, including lunch. We left on the bicycle. When we got off the paved road and into the village, Sam stopped at the chief's house to ask permission to park the bicycle there. The chief wanted to know whose kid I was and why I was going after little fish. Sam took the chief aside and they talked for a while. Then the chief came to me and said, "Bless you, little boy."

We walked to the rice fields. There were very narrow walkways that you had to walk through single file. Sam explained to me that the narrow walkways were to separate the rice fields and to regulate the water flow. He also told me which plants and bugs were good, and which to stay away from. There was plenty of water flowing through the fields.

It was a beautiful sight. Rice fields as far as you could see and mountains in the distance; even as a little boy it impressed me. We walked some more until Sam found a good spot to start fishing. Sam showed me how to tie the line to the hook, and how to bait the hook.

There was no reel on the pole just a straight line with a split shot about ten inches above the bait. Sam pointed out to me where to stand and how to throw the bait in the water. The first fish I caught was a catfish. Sam showed me how to take the fish off the hook.

Catfish have stingers. No matter how careful I was I always got stung. It hurt but I acted tough. We caught many fish that were all between four and six inches long. We also caught some catfish that were up to ten inches. Some of the big catfish swallowed the hook so we just cut the line and put the fish in the basket. We caught many fish, and then Sam told me it was time for lunch.

We found a good spot and Sam spread out the "tikar," which was a mat woven out of grass. After lunch we talked for a while; then I fell asleep. When Sam woke me up it was time to go home. It was getting too hot in the field. We walked to the chief's house. The chief was waiting for us because he wanted to see our catch. He said we did well and invited us for a cup of tea. We talked for a while, then Sam said, "It is getting very hot and I still have to teach this young man how to clean fish." The chief gave us permission to park the bicycle at his house anytime.

By this time my hand hurt, and it was swollen from the catfish stings.

At home Sam showed me how to clean the fish. My father checked on us and liked what he saw. He said, "Now you can go fishing on your own." Sam gave the fish to the cook and we ate fried fish at dinner. I did not tell my father, but I showed my mother my hand because it was swollen, and I was in a lot of pain. My mother was going to take me to the doctor the next day, but in the morning the swelling and the pain were almost gone. Finally, I told Sam that I got stung many times. He said he knew and that I was a tough little man. He also said that I was not very allergic to catfish stings.

When I went fishing by myself Sam made sure that I had plenty of fishing gear. The first time I was overwhelmed because I was all alone in such a big open space and there was nobody to talk to or to help me. I went to the different fishing spots Sam showed me and I started talking to Sam like he was there because I missed him. When I came to the village there were two little boys waiting for me. They followed me around and I asked if they wanted something. "Yes," they said, "we want to see the fish you caught." Then I asked if they wanted the fish. "Yes," they said. I gave them the basket with fish, and they ran home with it. I picked up my bicycle and I went to their house to get my fish basket back. Their mother was waiting for me and said that she could not keep the fish because she had no money. I told her that I did not want any money and that she could keep the fish; all I wanted was the fish basket back. The next time I went fishing the boys were waiting for me. Again, I gave them the fish, but when I got to their house their father was home and he invited me to come in his house. He asked me why I go to all the trouble of catching fish just to give it away. I said, "Because I don't need it, I make the boys happy, and it makes a good fish dinner for your family." I asked him what kind of work he did. He said he was a day laborer, but today was a bad day because there was no work. This is when I saw how poor this family really was. Their house was built from bamboo and had dirt floors. The house had four rooms, two bedrooms, four chairs, a kitchen with a bamboo bench and some storage space, a front and back door only, a roof made from coconut leaves, and no bathroom. It had no running water or electricity.

I fished a few more times, but then one day there was no water. I went home and told Sam that there was no water in the rice fields. Sam explained to me that when the rice was getting ready for harvest, they stopped irrigating the fields. I wanted to know where the fish went. Before they stopped irrigating, the villagers would harvest what they could, and the rest became fertilizer.

GETTING ACCEPTED BY THE (DESSA) VILLAGE PEOPLE

BY NOW EVERYBODY IN the village knew me; they were always very friendly and helpful, but I still felt like an outsider. One day I watched the boys play soccer. They played barefoot, and even though I had shoes on they invited me to play anyway. It was remarkable how well they played with a ball that did not even bounce. The ball was made from newspaper and rags and was held together with strings. We played until the ball fell apart. We always had a lot of fun and a lot of teasing went on. There was one older boy in the group who was the leader and kept the discipline among them. This boy seemed to know more of the people from where I came from because his father was a shoe repairman. Every day he took his tools with him and went house to house in the better neighborhood to find work.

One evening after we did our homework, I asked my father if I could have an old soccer ball for the boys in the dessa. We had maybe a dozen or so in the house for our own soccer teams. My father did not want to give any soccer balls to the boys from the village. He also told me not to go to the village and play with those kids anymore, but I continued to play in the village with my friends. Only Sam knew where I was. At home I would try to find materials like newspapers and old clothes to make a soccer ball for us to play with, but I had to do it without my parents knowing about it. Sam was always very helpful, but sometimes we played without a ball.

When the weather was hot the boys would go swimming in the river. I was afraid of deep water because I could not swim, but my friends taught me how. After swimming in the river, I had to make sure to take a shower. My father would get really angry if he found out that I was swimming in the river. I got caught many times and I was punished for it.

One day Sam told me he had to throw away two damaged soccer balls and he told me where he put them. I picked them up, looked them over, and in my opinion, it was a waste to throw them out. I took the damaged balls to the village and showed them to the boys, and one of the boys said his father could fix them. The shoemaker looked the balls over and said that the balls were damaged badly, but he would repair them. Every day we asked the boy if the balls were repaired. The boy said, "My father will let me know, do not ask." When the man finally called us to his house, he said he was sorry because he could only repair one ball. When he showed us the ball, we were all very surprised. I did not know what he did with the leather, but the soccer ball looked brand new. He made us feel like a real soccer team. I was amazed how hard and accurate these boys could kick with their bare feet using the new soccer ball. The boys practiced hard, but only in dry weather because they did not want the ball to get wet. I only came when I could.

After I thought the village players had improved, I talked to one of the coaches of my team to see if the kids from the village could play against us. He said no because playing against bare feet players was not fair. I asked my father, but he had already heard from the other coach. I told my father that the village players needed soccer balls and uniforms, but that they would give our team a hard time. My father said that it was impossible for them to win against players with shoes, shin guards, and organized by excellent coaches.

One day when I was practicing with the village team there was a well-dressed man watching us. I asked the boys who he was. They told me that he lived on the other side of the village. He was rich by their standards, and he worked in the city for the white folks. After practice the man took me aside and asked me why I wanted these boys to play against my own team. I explained that the village boys were very good, and my team was the strongest in my neighborhood. If the village players could prove themselves I hoped my father would give them better equipment. The man said that win or lose the game would be bad for me and that I should forget about the idea.

One day during practice the man showed up again, but this time he called us all together and tried to talk us out of playing my neighborhood team. The village players wanted to play, but my team had not accepted it yet. The man asked, "There are only fifteen of you, how can you practice if you don't have two full teams?" We explained, that we always played seven players against eight. The man said he would coach us, but we would have to listen because our team had a long way to go if we wanted to play against the white neighborhood kids.

Weeks went by and I did a lot of other activities with the boys. We practiced with our coach, whom we called Tim. He showed many things we did not know. I never asked him how he knew so much about soccer. We all accepted his teachings. Our ball was not holding up much longer, so Tim made us practice without a ball. We did a lot of running. Tim explained that if we ever wanted to have a chance of scoring we would have to outrun the other players all the time and make as little contact as possible with their shoes.

One day after practice with my own neighborhood team the young coach asked me if I still thought that "my team," the village team, could beat his team. It was as if I didn't belong to his team anymore. I said, "I don't know about winning, but they will give your team a run for the money." When I came to the village, I told Tim about what my coach had said to me. Tim wanted more time to help the village players prepare, and he also told me that I would not play against my own team. I was very disappointed, but he said he needed me to help with practice. When we practiced Tim made me put on my real soccer shoes and shin guards. He let me have the ball a lot so the other players could learn to take the ball away from me without coming in contact with my shoes. I was a good player and I gave them a hard time. After the boys got used to playing against someone wearing shoes, Tim played us seven against eight with a lot of running and short possessions of the ball.

Most of the fathers and coaches were not in my neighborhood anymore; they were called up for military duty in World War II. I told the young coach that we were ready to take them on. The coach said that he would let me know when the game would take place and that he would pick the field. I still played with my own team. After we scored the most points in our league, the coach told me that we would play the village team that Sunday at 3:00 p.m. This would be the hottest time of the day, and we only had enough players to have two subs for ninety minutes of play. With only fourteen players on the village side it worked out well for my neighborhood team. The field he picked was at the other side of the town. It was a very long walk for the village team. I told my players to meet me at the edge of the village at 11:00 a.m.. To my surprise all fourteen of them were wearing white T-shirts and black shorts. I asked them where they got them from, and they said Tim had supplied them.

"Let's have lunch," I said. I paid for it. Tim showed up after lunch and asked why we must leave so early. "It is a long walk," I said. However, Tim had already taken care of transportation. When we got to the field there was nobody there yet. Tim gave us last-minute instructions then disappeared. It was a helpless feeling without Tim. When the other team showed up, they had a lot of parents, coaches, friends and refreshments with them. We had nothing. The coach came over and asked if we had a coach. I told him we did not. He said to me, "You be the coach for this match." I had to make all the decisions for my players. Tim had this all figured out.

We won the toss-up. We had possession of the ball, but after the whistle blew one of my players got kicked in the shin. I had to replace him. We played hard, but in the beginning the other team had possession of the ball most of the time, because of their shoes. Right before halftime, we scored with a long ball from the corner. After the break, the other team had the ball. Another accident happened to one of my players. He lost the toenail from his big toe and it was bleeding badly. I ripped my T-shirt up and put pressure on the wound with it. A mother from the other side came over and gave me some ice. She helped me bandage the wound and told me to put some ice on the player with hurt shin as well. Then Tim's training started to pay off. We could outrun the other team now and had more possession of the ball, but we could not score. The defense made their shoes work for them, but I think the heat got to them. We scored another point. After the game was over there were no handshakes or congratulations and we left quietly.

There were a lot of sore feet, scrapes and bruises on my players, but they were all happy. I don't think that we could have done it without Tim's help. Tim picked us up and took us back to the village. We were the talk of the town, and in the village. Now, the village people treated me as their hero and made me feel welcome. However, where I lived nobody would talk to me about the game. It was as if it did not happen. I asked the coach about the reward. He said the village kids would get their reward as promised. It took weeks, but that was good because the village kids had to heal up anyway. Now they had two brand new soccer balls to play with. We got many invitations from other teams to play against them. Tim said we would play any team if they would take their shoes off, but we had no takers. I still played with the team in my neighborhood against other teams, but things had changed. The people – teammates, parents, friends, and coaches – were still friendly and talked to me, but there were no more invitations to birthday parties or other functions.

THINGS I DID AND LEARNED FROM MY NATIVE FRIENDS

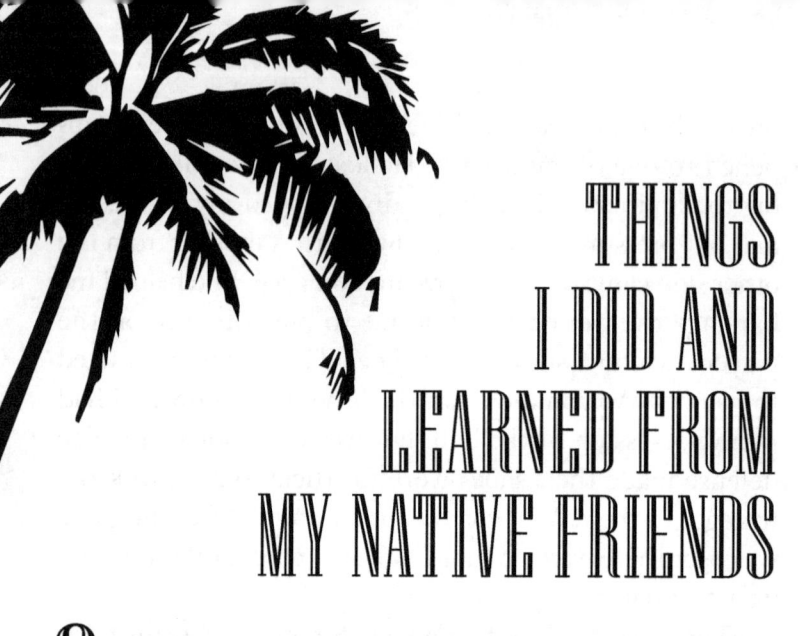

ONE DAY MY VILLAGE friends took me down to the river. The river was wide, deep and dirty. The villagers did everything in the river: bathed, washed their clothes, brushed their teeth, etc. The village had no sewer system, and all the run-off went into the river. They made a pipeline from hollowed-out bamboo that took water from a spring in the hillside to a place in the village. There were also some deep wells in the village. The well water was used for drinking and cooking.

The boys went downriver where there was an island. One side of the river was very wide and deep, while the other side was narrow and shallow. We went swimming, and after swimming the boys started cleaning up the shallow part. I wanted to know why they were cleaning the shallow water. They explained it was to catch fish because in the rainy season the river would rise, and the island would be mostly underwater. I had to go home to take a shower and do my homework before my father came home.

The next time I came down to the river I saw what the boys had done. They left the part upriver shallow and put branches in weighed down with rocks. As we went downstream the water got gradually deeper with depressions in between. At the end they had dammed the river with boulders and rocks. Now their trap was waiting for the rains. When the rains came the villagers knew that there would be a lot of fish in the trap. When the water was low enough to harvest their catch, there were lots of fish, eels and shrimp in the trap. The part of the catch that they could not eat right away they salted and dried in the sun.

Downriver there was a big rock on the bank that stuck out into the river. On one side of the rock was fast and deep water, and behind the rock was a big eddy. When the river was at a regular water level the rock towered out above the water. We often climbed the rock to jump in the fast water and swim underwater towards the eddy. The villagers played a game to see who could stay underwater the longest. During high water there were logs floating by the big rock. The boys waited on the rock until there was a log floating by that they could jump on to ride into the circling water behind the rock and get off of before the log went into the rapids. I did not play that game.

At the edge of the village was a store run by a Chinese man, whom I called Ming. Ming had anything and everything, new or used, in his store. One day I was looking for rope in his store. I found the rope I wanted, but I did not have enough money to pay for the rope. Ming wanted to know what I needed the rope for. I told him about the logs floating in the river. He said I could have the rope if I could get three logs on the bank for him. The next day we went to the river. The water had dropped a little, but the logs were too far away for us to get them to shore. It rained that day, and by the next morning the water level was just right, but no logs were coming downriver. Out of boredom my friends went swimming. I stayed on the lookout for logs. I fastened one end of the rope to a tree. Finally, a log came drifting by. The strongest swimmer tied the rope to the log and four of us on the riverbank pulled as hard as we could on the rope to get the log into the shallow water where we could secure it. That day we got three logs, so the rope was ours as Ming had promised. We were tired so we all went home.

The next morning, we got two more logs, but we wanted one more, so we waited a long time before one came drifting by. This log was a big one. Normally we wouldn't tackle one that big, but with the rope we thought we could do it. When our swimmer fastened the rope, we knew we were in trouble. We pulled as hard as we could, but we could not bring the log to the shallows. We let go of the rope and the rope broke. The log and rope both went downriver through the rapids. We were tired and our hands were very sore. We were all disappointed when we went home. We told Ming what had happened to the rope. He sent somebody down to cut the logs into firewood. Ming paid us and offered us more rope, but we refused.

Now that we had money, we had to decide what to do with it. The oldest boy suggested that we save all the money we earned, so that when we were grown up we could start a fish farm with the money. We had no clue how much that all would cost. I kept the money we had made so far, but I could not keep the money at my house. If my parents found out I would be in big trouble. None of the boys would keep the money at their place either. I suggested we talk to the chief to see if he might keep the money for us. The chief suggested the money could be kept at his house, but that I would be responsible for it. The chief gave me a wooden box and a key to a metal box and said from now on you are responsible for the money. The native kids did not go to school but had a lot of work to do in the village. Every day they had to find firewood for cooking, and find grass and brush for the sheep, goats and water buffalo. They had to work in the fields and tend to the gardens.

We would always meet in front of Ming's store. One day as I was waiting for my friends, Ming showed me his new aquarium. It was a big one. Then he showed me the fish he had for sale. I asked him how much he sold his fish for. He said from four for a penny to a dime apiece. I pointed out to him that I could catch some of the fish he had and asked how much he would pay me. He said he would pay a penny for ten live fish. When my friends showed up, I told them about the fish that Ming would buy from us. There said there were no fish like that in the river. I told them that I knew a place where we could find fish, but that we would need a net to catch them.

One of the boys said his father could help us because he used to be a hunting guide for the white folks. He could trap any wild bird or animal. When we returned to the village I talked to this boy's father, whom I called Jim. He said that what his son had told us was true, but that he would not do it for us. I told Jim about the fish Ming would buy from us, and that I knew where we could find them. Jim wanted to know where we could find them, and I told him it was on railroad property. Jim said that it was trespassing and that the police would pick us up. I told Jim that is why we needed a net. If we were to catch the fish by hand it would take us a long time and we would get caught for sure. Jim said he would think about it.

I began scouting on the railroad property to see where the fish were and where we could get in without being seen. The workers at the railroad knew who I was and paid no attention to me. Jim made me promise never to tell anybody about him. He knew that the village boys would not rat on him. Then Jim said he needed mosquito netting. I went home and told Sam that I needed mosquito netting and what it was for. The next day after school Sam told me that he had some netting put away for me. When I gave the netting to Jim, He said, "Your man must know what I am making." In my mind Sam knew everything. After my father left to play soldier Sam always helped me with my schoolwork.

When the net was made Jim called us to his house and asked us how we would go about catching the fish. I said we would just go in the water and net them. Jim said, "You guys don't know anything. First, you must learn their habits. Then net them when it's in your favor. I will teach you guys how to go about it." We never told Jim what kind of fish we were after, but he seemed to know.

Then Jim began talking directly to me because I could get on railroad property without being kicked out. Jim said, "In the morning the fish are in the shallow water and in the afternoon they are in the shadows in deeper water. Now go up there and find the spot where the most fish hang out." I checked in the morning and in the afternoon and found many places where the fish gather.

Then Jim said, "You guys have to listen real good." He gave us another net we needed. Then he explained what we needed to do. Jim said, "Get on the property without being noticed, then two of you go in the shallow water with one net and put it down first. Then, two of you go slowly in the deep water and put the net down. The fish will scatter but will come back to the deeper water. You might catch some in the shallow water. You have to hold real still until all the fish are back to the same spot, even as the mosquitoes and flies bite you in the face and arms. You also need the same water from the creek to transport the fish as quickly as you can." I brought mosquito repellent from my home and it worked. With one scoop of the net we caught lots of fish. We took the fish to Ming's store, and he was surprised that we got that many fish. Ming told us to come back tomorrow. The next day Ming had thrown out the dead fish and gave us money. He told us he did not need more fish.

Next Ming showed us doves and pigeons he had in the store. He said if we could bring him some of the birds, he would give us five cents a bird. The next day, I brought Ming two pigeons from home, and he paid me. I went to Jim and told him about the birds. Jim smiled; he seemed to enjoy helping us. I told Jim that I knew where there were many more birds and they were not afraid of people. "I know how to catch them," Jim said. However, he also told us at the moment he had no time to make the traps for us, and he would let us know when he did. While we were waiting for the traps my friends and I were scouting for places to set them. We did not know what the traps would look like. Jim said he needed the material to make the traps. I told him to tell me what he needed, and I would get it for him. Jim asked for big brown paper bags, buttons, and string. I must have given Jim a dumb look. Jim smiled and said just get me the stuff.

At home, I asked Sam how Jim could catch birds with paper bags. Sam did not know, but he got me twelve brown paper bags out of my father's office. I gave Jim the bags. "Now, I need twenty-four buttons," while he showed me the size, "and lots of string," he said. Then he sent me to scout more locations to place the traps. Jim also told us where to look for the birds. We looked at the park, behind the mosque, at the railroad station and the warehouse. The railroad warehouse where they stored corn, rice, and other grains was our best bet because there were not many people. Jim called us to teach us how to work the traps. Jim had stiffened up the bags with some glue. Then he glued two buttons on each side of the front of the bag. He fastened the string on one side to the buttons and through a hole in the buttons on the other side. Then, he put the bag on its side, put a small rock in the back, and gave me the string. He told me to walk about ten steps in front of the bag and pull on it slowly. The bag closed, and we understood how to work the trap.

Before we set the traps, Jim wanted to give us more instructions. He told us that all five of us must carry a trap, but only two would set it, and the other three would hang around close by. He told us to make sure and put some bait in and around the bag. If it was a little windy, we had to put a little rock in the bag. Jim told us that after we caught the birds we could leave together, but then all go in different directions to Ming's store. We wanted to know why. Jim said, "Sometimes the police are on the lookout for what you guys are doing and it's more difficult for them to catch you. If you can't get away, let the birds go before the police can grab you, then they only will take the traps away from you." We did it the way Jim taught us. We caught many birds at different places and did not get in trouble with the law.

Sometimes I went squirrel hunting using a slingshot with one of my native friends. We sat in a coconut/banana plantation, since this was where the squirrels traveled. We were sitting under a coconut tree, and it was very hot. There was no wind and no squirrels. In the distance there was a storm developing. It got very dark and we could see and hear thunder and lightning. My friend said, "We better not sit under this tree. The storm will be here soon, we better sit between the big boulders by the creek." He cut a couple of banana leaves to shield us from the rain. On these trips the native kids would always carry a knife, sickle, or a machete with them. It rained very hard and suddenly, we heard a big bang. We looked up and a fireball came down the hill straight at us, but it went in the creek next to us. Up on the hill a coconut tree was hit by lightning and completely destroyed. It stopped raining, the sun came out and we went home.

Jim's son told us that his father wanted to see us. That afternoon after school the boys and I went to his house. Jim was sitting in the shade in front of his house and invited us to come sit down. He said, "Look down into the valley, what do you see?" I said, "Cornfields and soybean fields." "Exactly," Jim said, "And they are ready to be harvested." He explained that after the crop was harvested, we would have a short time to catch many birds. "The traps you made for us will not work in the fields," I said. "That's right," Jim said. Jim had invited us over to teach us how to catch the birds.

Jim told us to go to the women in the village who make baskets from coconut leaves. He told us to ask for or buy the spines from the coconut plant. Jim wanted as many as we could get. The women in the village did not want to give us the sticks, but when we mentioned that Jim needed them, they gave us all the sticks we needed. Jim checked the sticks. Then we had to cut them all in different lengths. I had to pick out the long ones. Then

Jim took us down to the woods. On the way he made us pick up a piece of banana tree. In the woods Jim picked out the tree that had the pitch he needed. Jim cut some grooves in the tree and showed us how to put the pitch on the sticks. He told us to be careful not to get the pitch on our clothes or hair because it does not come off. The boys and I knew about this tree sap because we caught cicadas with it. The pitch did not dry up or wash away, it stayed sticky. I did not get to finish the job because it was getting late and I had to go home.

The next day after school the boys showed me the birds they caught. Jim made a special cage for the birds. We took the birds to Ming's store. He took the birds but did not give us the money we agreed on. I was not happy with this, but Ming said the birds were not in good shape because they had some feathers missing. When we got back to the village, I told Jim about Ming and that I was unhappy with it. The birds we were catching would always have some feathers missing. "Let's concentrate on catching more birds," Jim said. He walked down to the fields with us and picked out a spot for us. "There will be many birds coming down to this field," he said. Then Jim left, and the boys were showing me how to put the sticks down in the ground. We used part of the banana trees, and we had to make sure they were not too tight, and we couldn't put them where the ground was too hard. After all the sticks were put down it looked like a patch of tall grass.

The next morning was not a school day. The boys had to cut some banana leaves to lie on because Jim told us we had to lie face down in the field. When the birds were busy feeding, we all had to get up at the same time. The birds would fly into the sticks. The sticks would come loose, and the birds couldn't fly very well. This was our chance to catch them and put them in the cloth bags. We got some birds but most of them lost some feathers and flew away. We put the birds in the special cage Jim made and showed the birds to him. Jim said, "These birds lost more feathers than the ones we got yesterday." I asked Jim, "What if Ming does not want to pay us the money he promised?" "You let the birds go in front of him." "But then we won't get any money at all," I said. "It is better this way, the next time Ming will not go back on his word again," Jim said. We took the birds to Ming. I told Ming to look at the birds first. Ming said he had never seen such ugly birds, they looked like plugged chickens. "They're not worth two cents," he said, "but I will give you three cents a bird." I told him that we wanted what he promised. Ming said nobody would buy those birds from us. Nobody has to, I told him, and I let the birds go in front of him. Ming got very upset with us. We stayed away from Ming's store for a long time.

When the rice in the fields was ready for harvest there was a swarm of birds feeding on it. The villagers made little buildings from bamboo that stuck out above the rice fields. They fastened ropes to poles on the other end of the field with tin cans and colored ribbons tied to the ropes. When the birds would land on the rice fields the person in the hut would pull on the rope and the birds would fly up and land in the trees and bushes at the edge of the rice fields. We were waiting for the birds to shoot them with our slingshots. This would go on from dawn to dusk until the rice was harvested. The boys would always take the birds home and make a meal out of them.

After my father was called up for military duty in World War II the rules at home were not as strict anymore. After school, I did not stay indoors during the hottest time of the day. My mother did not know where I was or what I was doing. I always made sure to be home before dark by dinnertime. However, Sam knew, and he always made sure that I did my homework before I went to the village. Sam told me that education was the most important thing to have because once you have it, nobody could take it away from you. Sam was always there to make sure that I did things the right way.

On really hot days my friends and I went to play in the river to catch fish, eels and shrimp by hand. I stayed in the shallow area where I could catch fish and shrimp between the rocks and tall grass. The native kids went to the other side of the river where it was deep and where there were many holes in the riverbank. They caught big catfish and eels on that side. On days like this I would always come home with sore hands from the catfish stings. The native kids told me the way to take the soreness out was to pee on your hands. I did not believe them, but I did it anyway. One day we were catching fish again, and one of the boys caught a small iguana. We took the lizard to Jim. He told us it was a baby, and we should take it to Ming. Ming was happy to see us again. He took the iguana but did not give us any money for it. Ming asked us if we could catch iguanas of a certain size. If we could he would pay us good money, as much as twenty-five cents apiece.

The city garbage dump was down river from the village. There were many paths the iguanas would use from the water to the garbage piles. The river was very deep and wide over there and the current ran toward the dump side. We could not come in from the front because there was a tall cyclone fence with barbed wire over the top and a locked gate. Behind the gate there were two big incinerators with workers burning garbage all day and night.

We built a raft from banana trees and worked our way across the river. We put some snares out. The next day we checked the snares but did not catch anything. We went to Jim for advice.

We told Jim that Ming only wanted a certain size of iguanas, and he would pay us good money for it. Jim said it was very dangerous to cross the river over there. "We have a good system to cross the river," we said. Jim wanted us to explain how we did it. "We have built a raft from banana trees, then we tie a rope to a tree on both sides of the river, and we pull ourselves across the river," we explained. Then he asked us how we would make sure to catch the right size of iguanas with the snares. We did not know. Jim said, "When I build the traps for them, you cannot just put them anywhere. You have to go back up there and look for fresh runways," he explained. "How do we know they are fresh?" I asked. He explained that we had to look for fresh footprints and wet spots. The big ones did not use the same runways as the small iguanas. He told us that we needed to spread out and not speak to each other. We needed to look very closely at the riverbank where the iguanas were coming out of the water. Iguanas fed mainly at night, but you could always find some feeding at daytime.

We went up to the dump and followed Jim's instructions. We came up on some feeding iguanas and when they ran, we noticed the different runways they used. Back in the village we told Jim what we found. "But there are also many rats, birds and other animals up there," I said. The rats were a pest I was worried would steal the bait out of the traps. Then Jim wanted me to get him some tennis ball containers. They were made of metal in those days. Both my father and mother played tennis and I had to be the ball boy sometimes. Again, I asked Sam for the containers and told him what they were for. Sam told me that it was very dangerous in that part of the river and the fishermen who fish there at night believe that there are crocodiles in the river. But, as always, Sam got me the containers.

When I brought Jim the containers, I told him what Sam had said. Jim did not think that there were crocodiles in the river. Jim told me that the night fishermen might have seen big iguanas and mistaken them for crocodiles. Crocodiles and iguanas don't look alike; there is a big difference because iguanas have long necks and crocodiles have no neck. After Jim made the traps, he showed us how they worked. Jim cut the bottom out, then cut triangles in the containers, and pushed the sharp points inward. He left the lids on with a little hole through it, and a wire to fasten the bait and anchor the traps with.

Then, he told me to get some bait. "What do I have to get for bait?" I asked. "Get some raw beef, fish or chicken bones," Jim said. This took a bit of work. First, I asked Sam to get it from the cook for me. She did not want to give it to Sam. She told Sam that I had to ask her myself. When I did ask her, she wanted to know what I was up to. I told her the iguana story. She got upset and did not give me the bait. She thought that I was playing with neighbor boys. She thought it was not good for me to spend so much time in the village. "The village boys are always up to no good," she said. I did not say anything to her. The cook was like a grandmother to me. She worked for my real grandmother when my mother was still a little girl. After my mother got married, she was my mother's first servant and took good care of our family. I respected her.

In the village I told Jim about the cook and how she would not give me the bait. I told him I would get some money and buy bait at the market. "No," said Jim, "Here is where you guys have to use your smarts. Nobody needs to know what you guys are up to." He explained that there are always people who didn't like what we were doing. He told us to only work with people we trusted. "Iguanas eat cooked food too," Jim said. "When you have chicken or fish for dinner, save the bones," he told me. "And you boys, when the villagers butcher an animal, get some of the waste," he said. Sam was already ahead of me. Sam got me some raw bones and fish heads. In a short time, we had enough bait for all the traps. Jim showed us how to bait the traps, and made sure that we did it right, before he let us set the traps. Jim also said to make sure to put the traps by the right runways. We followed Jim's instructions very carefully when we set the traps.

The next morning, we wanted to check the traps, but Jim told us to give it more time. Two days later Jim told us to check the traps. To our surprise we caught two iguanas. We put them, trap and all, in our cloth bag and rushed to Jim's house. Jim was proud of us. He said, "You guys are learning the tricks of the trade." Jim took the animals out of the traps and put them in a wire cage he had made. Ming was very happy with our catch and paid us. "Bring some more," he said. We set the traps again. This time no iguanas, but the bait was always gone. Jim told us the rats got the bait before the iguanas. He told us to find a different place but stay out of sight. We found a good spot with many fresh runways. Jim did not help us bait the traps, but he checked them before we crossed the river. We waited four days before we checked the traps again. To our surprise there were three iguanas trapped. We went through the routine with Jim, and Ming still wanted more iguanas.

Jim warned us not to cross the river anymore because the rainy season had started, and it was already raining upstream. We took the rope off the trees and let the raft float downstream. Ming wanted us to get him some baby monkeys. Jim told us the only way to get baby monkeys was to shoot and kill the mother. We were kids, and we could not use guns.

The shoemaker's son told me that there was another store that had all kinds of birds, reptiles, and fish for aquariums for sale. He went inside and the storekeeper asked him if he wanted to buy something. He said no, but then he was asked to leave the store. My friend told me that I should go to that store and investigate. "You would not believe the prices in that store," he said. I put on my good clothes and went to the store. When I walked into the store the storekeeper walked up to me and asked me if I wanted to buy something. I said yes, but then the storekeeper asked me if there was an adult with me. I told him I had my own money I could spend. I could not believe my eyes when I saw the prices in that store. Customers came in, and that gave me more time to look around. The prices did not seem to bother them; they paid without complaint. It was an upscale store, where everything was clean and well taken care of. In the village my friends wanted to know how it went in the store. I said, "It went very good, I left on my own."

We all went to Jim's house and told him about the store and the prices in the store. "If we could do business with that store, we will make lots of money," I said. I asked Jim if he knew a way to get business from them. Jim looked at me but did not say anything. My friends were leaving, but Jim told me to stay. After the boys left, Jim told me that I was the one who could get the business. I told Jim that the storekeeper would not talk to me without an adult. Jim told them that first I needed to find out who the owner was, then become a familiar face in the store to build their trust. I spent a lot of time in the store and asked many questions.

One day, I came in the store and the storekeeper was talking to a well-dressed man. I did my usual rounds in the store, and then the storekeeper introduced me to the owner of the store. He said, "This boy comes here a lot but never buys anything." The storeowner asked for my name. Then he asked me if I was the son of and mentioned my father's name. I said, "Yes." Now things were getting a lot better. The owner told me that most of the critters in his store did not come out of the wild. This was 1940, and I did not know anything about conservation. The owner asked me what I was most interested in. "The pretty birds," I said. He wanted to show me where they came from and he took me to the back of the building. There were all kinds of cages for the birds and aquariums for the critters and fish. The workers had uniforms on, which was not common in those days. He asked me if I knew the name of the birds. I mentioned all the local names of the birds of our island of Java. "You know a lot about birds," he said. "I studied them in the wild," I said. "You never need birds out of the wild?" I asked. "Only when we need new blood," he said. I did not understand. He pointed to a cage and said, "We need new male birds in that cage." "I can get those birds out of the wild for you," I said. "What will you charge for it?" he asked. "Whatever the going price is," I said. "I will let you know," he said.

I went to Jim and told him that we might do business with that store. Jim said, "I am already working on the trap to catch adult birds." The trap, as best as I can

Things I Did and Learned from My Native Friends

remember, was made of bamboo and soft wood. It was a two-level cage, and the bottom part was for the bait. The top had two compartments, and the trapdoors opened upwards with only the trigger stick inside the trap for the bird to land on. Jim told me to start scouting for the birds that the store wanted. He told me to go to the edge of the woods by the farmers' fields. There were many different birds with their own territory. I scouted for days, but I did not have time to see my friends.

When I went back to the village, I saw my friends, and asked them why they were not working with me. They said Jim told them not to, but they did some business with Ming and gave me the money. I asked Jim why the boys could not work with me. Jim said he meant for the boys to not go with me to the store run by the white people. We did some business with Ming, and I still did my visits at the other store. With permission I could go in the back and look at all the animals and get to know the workers.

One day when I came in the store the owner was waiting for me. He said he needed two male birds. I told him I could do that, but I needed one of his male birds. The owner did not like that at all. He must have been thinking that this was a way for me to get an expensive bird for nothing. However, Jim had me well prepared and I told the owner that I would pay him the full amount for his bird, but that he would need to buy all three birds back from me. There were also conditions before he would buy the birds. They had to be quarantined. I did not know what that was. The owner explained to me that if I could catch the birds and bring them in, they would be put in a cage away from all the other animals for a while. They would be checked for diseases and if they were very old, I would have to release them in the wild again. I agreed to the conditions, paid for the bird and left.

When I got to the village, I told Jim about my agreement with the store. Jim said, "You pulled it off." "But I paid for the bird," I said. "That does not matter, you won their trust," Jim said. I had to go home. Jim set the trap for me. The next day after school I went to Jim's house and he had already put the birds in a cage with three separate compartments. I was surprised and very happy. "Jim, you are the best trapper in the world," I said. "I know a lot about animal behavior," he said. Then he told me how he caught the birds so quickly. Male birds are very territorial early in the breeding season and that is how we got the upper hand.

When my friends and I made some money we always offered some to Jim. The only money Jim asked for was for the material to make the traps. I think that the chief and Jim had a talk. I took the captured birds to the store. The storekeeper could not believe what he saw. He said, "You got the order yesterday afternoon, and you are bringing us the birds already. You must know a lot about catching wild birds." I said, "I just got lucky." The storekeeper sent a worker to get the owner. The owner was surprised that I caught the birds already. He looked the birds over and told me they looked like nice young birds. "I will put the birds in quarantine and let you know what I think in two weeks," he said. After ten days the storeowner called me over and told me he had something for me. He gave me an envelope with money in it. "They are nice birds and I will keep them," he said. I did not open the envelope, but instead went straight to Jim's house to open it there. My friends and I had never made so much money all at once. "Bring the money to the chief," Jim said. I did, but the chief told me to put the money away; he did not want to see it.

We did a lot more business with Ming. We also caught grasshoppers, crickets, grubs, and other insects. He also wanted baby mice and rats, specifically the newborns that were still hairless and blind. Ming always had business for us, but the pay was very low. One day when I came in the pet store the owner showed me scorpions, big black ones, we called them bleu scorpions, and told me the ones he got out of the wild didn't live long. If I just could get him two that would live, he would pay me very well. "Those are dangerous critters," I said. "That is why I will pay you good, but they have to stay in quarantine for a long time," the storeowner said. I went to Jim's house and told him what the storeowner told me. Jim smiled and looked at me. I think that Jim really liked me because I was growing up together with his son. Then he said, "If you can keep this man as a customer, you could make lots of money." "What about the scorpions?" I asked. Jim said, "The story goes that one sting of those scorpions can kill a horse." "Is it true?" I asked. Jim laughed and said, "I never have seen a horse get stung." Then he told me to get the boys.

We went to the woods and Jim asked us to show him where we saw the scorpions. We showed Jim the place and found some scorpions. Jim told us to look at the hole the scorpion lies in. He explained that the holes are not round, and they are flat. The scorpion barely fits in the hole for protection. Jim then told us to look for the path from the scorpion's hiding place to his hunting grounds. We could not find any, then Jim pointed out to us what to look for. "Leave these alone, I will take you to where the big ones are," Jim said. Jim took us to a hill in the woods and said, "Look at this hill, do you see any difference?" We shook our heads. Jim explained that one side is drier, and scorpions like the drier side of the hill where there is a lot of dew at night. "Now, let's see if we can find any," Jim said. There was a lot of evidence that there were scorpions living there, but we did not see any. Jim did not want us to disturb them. On the way home Jim told us why the scorpions at the pet store died after a short time. The people who caught them used poison gas to get them out of the crevices in the rocks. "But we will get the man healthy ones," Jim said.

Back at the village Jim told me to get him green bottles, not the real dark ones, but the ones you can see through. Jim told me the size of the bottles that he needed. At home, I told Sam that I needed the bottles and what they were for. Sam said, "We don't have them at the house, but go to your father's clubhouse and ask the bartender." The bartender told me to look in the storeroom. He also wanted to know what I needed the bottles for. I gave him a story. I remember Jim telling us never to tell anybody what we were doing. I took the bottles to Jim, and he told me to come back in a few days.

Jim also worked. I don't know where he worked, but sometimes he was gone for days, and sometimes he was home. I suspected that he worked for the railroad because he knew a lot about my father. I told the storeowner that I could get him healthy scorpions. "It will take a while, they are hard to get," I said. "They will not die in a few days," I added. The storeowner said, "I believe you." The traps were very simple. Jim cut the neck off the bottles, which made the entryway large. Then he put some straw or hay inside the traps, then he put some crickets in a small wire cage in the back of the trap. Jim went with us to set the traps because he wanted to make sure that we did it right. After the traps were set, Jim said there might be some other people looking for scorpions at night, so somebody had to stay overnight. "Maybe not, it's too far into the woods, but you boys have to get here early in the morning before it gets too warm," Jim said. The critters have a hard time crawling out of the trap, but when it gets too hot, they might succeed. Jim was talking to my friends, he knew that I had to go to school in the morning. Jim gave the boys corks made from soft wood with small holes in it. "When there is a scorpion in the trap, make sure to put the cork on tight before you take the trap out," Jim said.

The next day after school I could not wait to get to Jim's house. The boys were standing outside Jim's house. I asked them if we caught any scorpions. "Yes!" they said, but Jim went with them and handled everything himself. I said, "We are very lucky that we have Jim." He handled the scorpions himself because he did not want any accidents. Jim called me inside and showed me two big scorpions in clear glass jars. Jim told me scorpions didn't like too much daylight and if you expose them to it, they will die. I put the jars in a pillowcase and took them to the pet store. The storeowner examined the critters really well and said, "They are beautiful, I hope they will live." "I guarantee it!" I said.

The most difficult bird for us to catch was the wild chicken. They lived in the thick underbrush in the woods but fed in the open at the edge of the woods and in the farmers' fields. The hens had green, yellow, brown and black feathers. The chicks were brown, and the roosters had long red and blue combs, long tails, and many different colored feathers. They lived in small groups from one rooster and one hen to one rooster with twelve hens. The hen usually separated herself from the group to raise her brood. Jim told us not to put the traps in the farmers' fields or at the edge of the woods. We always found birds feeding in the open places or on the hillside in the distance, but when we came close to their feeding grounds they disappeared. We could hear them in the underbrush, but we could never see them. The birds could fly but preferred to run. It was very frustrating for us to be fooled by these birds all the time, but with Jim's help over a long period of time we managed to trap four birds: one rooster and three hens. They were young birds from many different groups. The pet storeowner was very happy with the birds and paid us lots of money for them.

When the tropical fruits were ripe the fruit bats came out at night to feast on them. There were some big ones called flying foxes. The local native name is kalong. My friends and I were shooting at them with our slingshots. No luck, they were up too high in the trees. We asked Jim for help. Jim said, "The best way to get them is with a spotlight and a rifle, but I don't want you boys in the woods after dark anyway." He knew that I had to be home by dark. A lot of the fruit bats came out just before dark, and we kept trying to catch them with no result. The oldest boy said, "We're shooting at the bats too early. They are still too high in the trees and it will be dark before they come back." He explained, "There is a lot of ripe fruit on the lower branches, and if we wait, they will come to get this fruit." We waited, but no bats came, only mosquitoes that were feasting on us. The next day, we were at it again. We waited, and no bats, but no mosquitoes because I brought repellent from home and it worked. The fruit on the higher branches was almost gone. The bats had to come down to the lower branches where the ripe fruit was. My friends cut some banana leaves and other big leaves and wrapped the fruit on the lower branches in them, so the bats couldn't get to the fruit. We did this because we could not stay after dark, and we could not see the black bats in the dark anyway.

The next day, we came a little earlier to take the wrapping off the fruit. There was hardly any fruit left on the tree except on the branches we wrapped. My friends gave me the honor to have the first shot. We took our position. We didn't have to wait long. A big bat landed on a low branch with ripe fruit. The bat folded its wings and started eating the fruit upside down. I aimed and hit the bat on the head. It dropped, but was not dead, so the boys killed it with a stick. It was getting dark, so we left and went to Jim's house to show him our catch. Jim's wife told us that Jim was at work and wouldn't be back for a week. I asked my friends to keep the bat and bring it to Ming the next day. The boys did not want to go to Ming without me and did not want to keep the bat overnight. I took the bat home.

Sam was waiting outside the house for me. Sam told me that my mother had asked him where I was. Sam said, "I told your mother that you were playing in the neighborhood, and that I would get you." He told me to be prepared when I went inside. I told Sam that we got a big bat and that the boys did not want to go to Ming without me. "Give the bat to me, and I will take care of it," Sam said. My mother did not ask where I was but said that I should know better than to stay out after dark. I did not say anything. I cleaned up and went to my room. The next day after school, I asked Sam what he did with the bat. "I wrapped it up and put it in the refrigerator," he said.

My mother would freak out if she found it, I told him. We were one of the lucky families who had a refrigerator in those days. Most families had iceboxes. We had an icebox as well. It was a wooden box lined with metal and a drain hole. Inside was a big piece of ice covered with sawdust. A servant would cut some ice in little pieces and put it in a thermos to be consumed with our drinking water. Sam told me to take the bat to Ming to find out if he wanted it. I asked Sam why he had cut off the wings. "I will tell you later," he said. Ming took the bat and gave me money for it, but Ming wanted to know why I cut the wings off. "I have other purposes for it," I said. I did not know what Sam's plans were yet.

When I got home, I told Sam that Ming wanted to know why I cut the wings off, "And, what did you say?" Sam asked. "I told Ming that we had another use for it," I explained. "Good," said Sam, "Now I'll tell you why I cut the wings off." He explained that we could make more money when we sold the wing bones separate. He said that we were very lucky that both wing bones could be used. These bats had a habit when they were not killed instantly to bite into their left wing, which crushed the bone and made them worthless. "Who will buy bare bones?" I asked. Sam explained that people who smoke would make cigarette holders out of them. Then he showed me the bones. They looked all clean to me.

Sam told me it was my job to ask my friends to clean the inside of the bones. "OK, I will ask them," I said. "Not those friends," Sam said. He took me to an anthill under a mango tree in our yard and said these are your friends. These ants were very aggressive, and they bit. Sam made a small hole on each side of the bone, tied the bone to a stick, and pushed the stick in the anthill with the bone not touching the ground. The ants were all over it in an instant. "These ants will clean the inside of the bone for you," he said.

The next day after school Sam told me to check on the bones, and if they were clean to bring them to him. "How do I know that they are clean?" I asked. Sam told me they were clean when there were hardly any ants on them. I checked, no ants. I gave the bones to Sam, and he looked them over. He looked through the holes and said they were good, and he kept the bones. No more bat hunting for me though. I made sure to be home before dark. I didn't want my mother to be upset with me. I was talking to my neighbor and told him that I shot a big fruit bat with my slingshot. He was trying too but hadn't had any luck yet. He said that the boys down the street were shooting at the bats with a spotlight and a shotgun and were getting them. I asked him if he knew what they did with the bats they shot. I asked if he could get them if they didn't keep them. "What for? I don't want them," my neighbor said. "Give the bats to me," I said. "And what will you do with them?" he asked. "I give the bats to my houseboy," I said. Then I told him that I could not be outside after dark, but I would put a bucket next to the servants' entrance where he could put the bats when he got them.

I told Sam that the neighbor boy might bring us some bats and that I would put a bucket at this entrance. Sam told me to go in the house, and he would take care of it. I did not have the chance to talk to Sam until after school. Sam told me to thank the neighbor for the bats, then take them to Ming and come straight home to start my homework. Sam did not want me to go to the village. I did not say anything, but in my head, I thought, "Who are you to tell me what to do?" Sam knew that I was not doing very well at school, so he always made sure that I did my homework, and he helped me with it. We went through the same routine with the wing bones and the ants. Sam kept the bones.

That evening I met my neighbor in the front yard on the wall. All the houses in my neighborhood were owned by the railroad. Brick walls were used instead of fences to divide the properties. The walls were as low as four feet in the front yard and as high as eight to ten feet on the side and in the back. The high walls had broken glass cemented in to prevent kids from playing on them. My neighbor friend asked me if I wanted to go watch the older boys hunt bats. I still couldn't be outdoors after dark. My neighbor said he had a plan. He told me to ask my mother if I could play at his house that night. It was OK with my mother as long as I was in bed before 10:00 p.m. My friend introduced me to the hunters. The hunters were between fifteen and seventeen years old. They were much older than me, but they were nice guys. They were happy that I would take all the bats they shot. That night we did not shoot any bats, because most people would not give us permission to shoot on their property. We hunted along fences, the street, and on railroad property, but there was nothing to shoot. The next evening my neighbor friend came over again and asked my mother if I could play at his house. This time my mother said that I had to stay home. The next day after school Sam told me that he found another bat in the bucket, and that the bones were already on the anthill. I took the bat to Ming.

I went to the village and my native friends told me that Jim wanted to see me. We all went to Jim's house. Jim wanted to know why I had not come over for such a long time. "After school, Sam makes me do my homework; he is worse than my father," I said with a smile. "But I made some money," I added. I told them that in my neighborhood there were white boys who hunt for the big bats with a spotlight and a shotgun. I explained how my next-door neighbor brought me the dead bats and I brought them to Ming. I told them Sam took care of the wing bones. Jim treated us to young coconuts. Jim told me the boys had trapped some birds and geckos for Ming, but they didn't want to keep the money, so he had it. Jim also told me that Ming wanted us to catch dragonflies to feed to his captive birds.

"Where do we find the dragonflies?" I asked. "You have seen the swarms of those big orange dragonflies?" he responded. "Yes, but how do you catch them?" I asked. Jim told me the dragonflies were the farmers' friends. They would fly in big swarms in daytime and eat small insects. Then when the sun went down, they had to find a place to roost. Since there were so many of them, they would roost high up in the trees and in low branches of the shrubs in yards. "Now is the time to catch them; it is almost the rainy season," Jim said. "When the rains come, the dragonflies are gone," he added. Jim gave me a wire cage and told me to sit on my front steps before dark and to pay attention to where the dragonflies roosted. I had never paid attention to them before. When I did, I really found out how many there were. After dark with a flashlight Sam helped me collect them. We got a whole bunch of them. My native friends collected even more than I did. We took our catch to Ming. Ming looked at our catch and said, "That is too much, how can you boys catch that many dragonflies in one day? I can only keep a three-day supply." He took what he needed and gave us money.

I took what was left over to the pet store. When I walked in, the first thing the storekeeper said to me was, "Where have you been?" "I have been doing a lot of other things, mostly homework from school," I lied. "I brought you dragonflies, you can feed them to the birds and other critters," I said. "I have to ask the owner, he is in the back," the storekeeper said. When the owner came in the store, he asked me if the dragonflies were still alive. I showed him the cage. He said, "Let's go to the back and feed them to the birds and other critters." We talked for a while. I was really impressed how well the animals were taken care of. "I have to go," I said. The storeowner asked how much he owed me. "I did not ask for any money," I said. The owner said, "You have to be paid for catching the dragonflies." He gave me money, much more than what we got from Ming.

With the money from my native friends, the bat money and the dragonfly money, I had a lot of money to bring to the chief's house. The chief was home and asked me to come and sit with him at the table, and he offered me a cup of tea. We talked about many different subjects. Then he asked me what my plans were when I grew up. I told him my plan after high school was to go to Holland and study to become a doctor. Then I would come back and take care of my people. Unfortunately, that never happened.

THE EXCITEMENT OF KITE COMBAT

EVERY YEAR BEFORE THE wet season we had the aerial kite combat season. It was an adult sport. We, the younger kids, waited downwind with long sticks with branches on top, for the free-floating kites that had lost the battle and come back down to earth. When somebody could untangle the yarn of the kite in the branches of his long stick and run in the opposite direction, the kite became his. It was a free-for-all battle and many kites were ripped to pieces. We also tried to catch the yarn from the loser. Then we would tie it to a branch or tree and wait until it broke off. It was not fair, but it was the only way the native kids could fly a kite. The oldest of my native friends and I would go on my bicycle through the neighborhoods where the native kids didn't usually go. When a kite fell on someone's property, I would go to the house and ask if I could get the kite. Sometimes, they would ask if the kite was mine, and I would always answer yes.

At home, I talked to Sam about the aerial kite combat. I told him it looked like fun. He told me that anybody could fly a kite, but to become one of those aerial combat pilots took skill and a long time to learn. "I would like to learn it," I said. "You are a little young, but it is always good to learn," he said. "This is one thing I am good at," Sam said. I asked my mother for money to buy what we needed. My mother wanted to talk to Sam first. I heard her say to Sam you better not be making a gambler out of my son. Then she told me to get out of the room. Sam told me that he had to promise my mother that I would never bet on the kite fighting. My mother gave Sam money for the supplies we needed. Sam bought special paper to build the kites, glue, and sewing yarn. To make the abrasive line Sam had his own formula. I don't remember everything that went in it. I knew he used different pieces of glass that we had to grind up to a very fine powder, some tree bark, and other things. He mixed the ingredients together, added water to it and brought it to a boil away from the house because the glue had a very bad smell to it. While the formula was cooling off, Sam wound the yarn on another spool, then soaked it overnight in the formula.

The next day, I watched Sam loop the yarn around poles in the backyard. He held the yarn between his thumb and index finger with tree bark from a certain tree. Then, he slowly walked backwards so the drippings would fall back in the pan. After the yarn was dry Sam inspected the yarn really closely for any uneven spots in the application. If there were any, Sam would go through the whole process again. Sam made the spool from a can. He placed a round piece of wood inside the can, and then wrapped the can with paper. Then, it was time to put the abrasive line on the spool. This is when my lessons started. Sam showed me exactly how he wanted the abrasive line to be put on the spool. Sam made me finger protectors because the abrasive yarn could cut through skin before you knew it.

Sam took me for a bicycle ride to the different places where the kite fights were. Sam told me to look at all the different kites. He explained that the ones with tails and other ornaments on them were noncombatant kites. The high-flying diamond-shaped kites were the champions. Every kite had its own color patterns, and that was what Sam was checking out because we didn't want the same pattern when we came to fight them. At home, Sam started making the kite frames. He was so meticulous, everything had to be perfect. I was getting anxious to get out there and do combat.

It was vacation time, no school. Sam told me to go to the village and play with my friends. I went to Jim's house; he was sitting on his front porch. When he saw me, he asked with a smile what I was up to now that the boys were all running after kites. "I have tried that too, but there are too many people after one kite. I did it different," I told him. I explained that I had the the shoemaker's son pedal me on my bicycle through the better neighborhoods, so that when a kite fell on their property I went to the house and asked if I could pick up my kite. I told him it worked most of the time. Jim looked at me and smiled, "You're good," he said. "What I really came here for was to tell you that I was going to do kite combat with Sam," I said. "Aren't you a little young for that?" Jim asked. He explained that there was a lot of wagering going on among those people. "How do they do that?" I asked. Jim explained, "The high-flying kites challenge each other by maneuvering their kites a certain way. When the challenge is accepted the kites will pull up next to each other, waiting for the signal that the wagering is done, and the fight can begin." He told me the most skilled pilot would be awarded with the win. He told me the kites tried to attack from above, and the pilots would try to outmaneuver each other. Jim explained that it could take as long as fifteen minutes, but when the kites connected it did not take long for one of the kites to be free floating in the air. Then he said, the winning pilot was always given some money whether he had bet or not.

At home, Sam showed me the kites. He had built six of them. Our colors were black tops with red or green bodies. They looked a little bigger than the ones in the field. Sam told me he did that on purpose, and he would show me why when we tried them out. The next day, in the afternoon, when the wind was right Sam took me on the bicycle to railroad property. He asked permission, then took me to an open field where there were no kites flying. Sam told me I needed to listen really well. "You have to know how to hold the spool. When I pull the kite up, you hold the spool in front of you, then wind the yarn as fast as you can onto the spool," he said. He continued, "Never let any yarn touch the ground. When I am in combat and connect with the other line, I have to give line very fast because with any little obstruction the opponent will cut my line. You have to hold the spool in line with my elbow and you have to be very fast." Then he said he wanted to find out how fast I could learn. We put our finger protection on, then Sam put the kite in the wind and the kite went up with no problem. Then he pretended to be in combat and expected me to handle the spool well. Sam did not say anything; he was maneuvering the kite to my speed of handling the spool. After an hour or two, I asked Sam to quit. "My fingers and wrist hurt," I said.

On the way home, Sam said that I did good for the

very first time. The next day, he took me to the same place, but this time Sam let me play with the kite. He showed me how to make the kite turn left, turn right, go straight up, and dive. He also showed me how fast he could wind the line onto the spool. On the way home, I told him I wanted to go to the place where the action was the next day. Sam said I was not ready yet. It took five more two-hour learning sessions before I was ready.

The day finally came when we were going to the field to do combat with the other kites. Sam got me sunglasses and a wide rim hat. He told me to wear them at all times. When we got to the field there were small groups of people, all adults, around the kite pilots. Those were the people who would wager a lot of money against each other. Sam found a place to launch the kite. He gave me the kite and told me to get it up as high and as fast as I could. It went really smoothly. Then the trouble started. A man came to me and said, "This is not a place for a snot nose like you to fly a kite. Here we do serious kite flying," he added, "and I know where you live." I took a closer look and most of the men were from the better, white neighborhoods. "But I had permission from my mother, Sir," I said. In those days a child would never call adults by their first name unless it was a servant. "In a minute, you will lose your kite," he said.

We were flying high up, where only the super stars flew. A kite dove in our direction to cut our line, but Sam out-maneuvered him every time. Sam pulled our kite up ready for combat. None of the wagering people approached us. I didn't know if they wagered any money on our fight. Sam kept out-maneuvering the opponent until he had a chance to attack from above. Sam made a quick dive to connect and the other kite was free floating in the air.

Everybody was surprised except Sam. He smiled and gave a thumbs-up. He made some victory dives, then put the kite straight up, ready to take on any of the kite pilots. The next opponent came up but did not attack right away. Sam told me they were betting. The signal was given, and the combat began. It was very interesting; both pilots wanted to attack from above, but I was so busy with the line and spool that I missed the fight. Sam told me it was over, and I looked up and saw the other kite floating away.

Sam handed me the line and told me it was time to take the kite down because we were leaving. A man came over and told me for a little boy I handled the kite very well. I looked at Sam but did not say anything. The man said, "I wish you did not take the kite down because there are more pilots who want to fight you." "It is no use; I already beat your best pilots," I said. Sam told me to be quiet. Sam took the kite off the spool and told me to carry the kite over my shoulder to show everybody that I was the champion that day. On the way home, Sam scolded me about the way I talked to the men in the field. "You're still a kid and they are not servants," Sam said. Then Sam explained why our kites were bigger than the others. He told me that when I was ready to fight and could get above the other kites to dive down and contact the opponent's line, it would cut the line every time I caught enough wind. But since our kite was so heavy from its size, if an opponent attacked us from above and we didn't give line fast enough they would cut us every time.

At home, Sam checked the line. He gave me the end to hold and told me to walk away slowly. He put the line between his thumb and index finger as I walked backwards. I wanted to see what he was doing, but then he said, "That is far enough," and he cut the line. "What do you want me to do with the line you cut off?" I asked. "Wind it on a spool and save it."

We went to a different place to look for combat. There were many kites already fighting in the air. Sam parked the bicycle and told me to stay there. I knew what he was doing; he was looking for a place where he can could catch a good wind. Sam motioned for me to come over with the kite. Sam told me to look where the high flyers were, and to take the kite up there. Our reputation had gotten ahead of us. While I was bringing the kite into position, some men from the crowd recognized our colors. They came over and said that they wanted to support me. I said, "I don't need any support, Sir." Sam said, "They want to bet on our kite fighting skills." "What is there for us?" I asked. "When you win, you will find out," the man said. After the first win, more people gathered behind us. The man gave me some money. I said, "Give it to my pilot, Sir." I don't know if Sam was betting or not. After winning four in a row, Sam took the kite down without checking the line, and said, "That is enough." I put the kite over my shoulder, we walked across the field and left.

At home, Sam wanted to give me some of the money, but I did not accept it. Sam told me he had never made so much money in one day. He told me he made more than his wages for a month. These people, mostly white, bet lots of money on the kites. I asked Sam why he never checked our line after a win. He told me he just had a feeling. "We have to make more abrasive yarn," Sam said. I told him I would ask my mother for more money, but Sam told me he had plenty. We went to another place with our fresh-made abrasive yarn. Sam knew all the places, and he picked the ones where there were many whites flying kites. Sam asked me to be polite to the grownups. I told him it didn't matter what they said to me, but I didn't like it. They were not any better than Sam and I. Sam asked me to just do him a favor and be polite.

When we walked up on the field, I heard some people say, "Here comes the Indonesian man with the white boy." I had never seen any of the people. Sam was looking for a place to launch our kite. I brought the kite up to where the champions were. The people who followed us were exchanging insults back and forth, and a lot of bad words were said. Then a man from the other group came over and started inspecting our spare kites, which was not allowed without permission. Our followers and the opponents were having words again. I gave the spool to somebody and walked over to the other group and started messing with their kites. Then a man grabbed me by the arm and said, "You are going to get a whipping you never had before." To prevent more trouble, a man from our side came over and got me. I was only ten years old. Sam said, "If you keep this up, I will take the kite down and we will go home." The people behind us did not want us to do that. Then, I said, "We will only do combat for a percentage." Sam gave me a dirty look. The men behind us told me not to worry; they already knew all about it. Because of the tension the wagering was heavy.

After the first win, Sam gave me the line and told me to try it. I tried to out-maneuver my opponent, but he got me from above. I barely felt the connection and my kite was already free floating in the air. Sam told me to bring the line in as fast as I could. There was a loud celebration, and many bad words from the other group. Sam inspected the line, cut off the worn part, then sent another kite up. I heard the other group saying that we were not all that good. Sam took all the money he earned from the previous kite fights and said he would wager that against anybody. This was the first time Sam had spoken during the combat. It must have been a big sum of money. There was silence for a moment.

After the matchmakers got everything straightened out (it took a little longer this time), the fight began. Sam looked at me and said, "You have to be at your best." The other pilot was very good too. It took many tries from both pilots. Sam pulled our kite up as fast as he could. I had a hard time keeping up with Sam. The other kite followed, but Sam was already above him. Sam caught a good wind, dove down to make contact and it was over. After the pay-off there was only silence. Sam took the kite down, inspected the line, and cut off the worn pieces. He brought the kite back up and made some challenging moves, but there were no takers. Sam gave the line to me and said, "Play with it for a while." "I am not fighting anybody," I said. Sam gave the spool to somebody and walked off. I think he was collecting his winnings. I was very nervous holding the line while Sam was away. I was afraid that those super pilots would attack me. They tried, but I stayed as far away from them as far as I could. Then I heard them hollering, "He is on the run!"

Sam came back and took over to challenge them, but now they were on the run. Sam gave the line back to me and told me to keep it up there. The matchmakers went all over the field to get a match going against us. When they came back there were no takers. Sam let me have the line a little longer; then he told me it was time to go home. With the kite over my shoulder I walked to the enemy's side and walked slowly past them out of the field. Sam was not happy with me. He told me if I ever caused trouble again, we would not do any more combat. The next morning, Sam told me to play in the village with my friends and to take the used yarn with me. The yarn for combat couldn't have any knots in it. Then he gave me three kites and told me I could fly the kites with my friends. "What is wrong with these kites?" I asked. "They are not perfect for combat, but they are excellent for you and your friends to play with," he said. "I have a lot of work to do," he added.

I went to the village and went by Jim's house. He was home, sitting on his front porch, and motioned for me to come over. He offered me a cup of tea, then asked me how the kite flying with the big boys was going. Before I could answer, Jim said, "I heard you are a troublemaker." "How do you know? I have not talked to anybody," I asked. "That kind of news travels fast," he said. "Where are the boys?" I asked. "They are doing their chores," Jim said; "they will be here soon." Jim and I talked about many different subjects. Jim asked me if I would work for the railroad when I grew up. I told him that I would go to Holland and study to become a doctor. As a ten-year-old, I had big plans.

The boys came over. They all had kites and yarn that they stole from the losing kites in combat. We went to a field by the river. We did not do any real combat, but we tried all the tricks of real combat. We would take the kite straight up, make it dive straight down, turn left, turn right, let it catch the wind, and make loops. We played until we got tired. I asked Sam when he would take me kite flying again. He said he had to take care of things at home first. I went to Ming to see if he had anything in mind for us. Ming said he had a lot of things for us to do. I told him he had to wait because we were catching kites. "That's all play," Ming said, "You boys have to think about making money." I told him, "Your pay is not very good, we're going to take some time out to play."

I went to the pet store and told them the same story about kite play. The owner took me in the back and showed me his new machine, an egg incubator, and told me that he was using the machine to hatch eggs. I said, "How can a box hatch eggs?" He told me to find some eggs out of the wild and he would show me. I said, "It's almost the rainy season, there are not many birds nesting now. What kind of birds are you thinking of?" I asked. He told me that first he wanted wild chickens, after that he wanted green pigeons, then house pigeons, and doves. I told him I didn't think any of those birds had eggs at the time. He told me only the house pigeons might have eggs. The owner said, "I would really like to try my machine out; bring me eggs of any of those birds, so that I can find out if the machine really works." "Is the machine also feeding the little hatchlings?" I asked. "No," he said, "We have a special formula and a special way to feed them."

At home, I asked the man who took care of our animals if there were any pigeons nesting. "Why are you asking?" he said. "I want some eggs," I said. "Don't take any eggs that the bird is already sitting on," he said. I found four pigeon eggs and took them to the pet shop. The owner was in the shop, so he let me test the eggs. When he came back, he told me the eggs were good. "What do you mean, are good?" I asked. "Fertile," he said, but I did not understand. The owner said, "In three weeks we will find out." The owner gave me some boxes that looked like egg cartons. They were made of wood with real soft padding inside. The owner told me not to take all the eggs out of a nest, but to always leave one or two in the nest, and to only take the fresh ones.

I went to the village and told Jim about the machine and the eggs that the pet storeowner wanted. I asked him if it was possible for a machine to hatch eggs. Jim said he didn't know, but that people were getting smarter all the time. I asked Jim, "How do I know when the eggs are fresh?" He told me when I found a nest to not just climb up a tree and take the eggs. He told me that instead I needed to check the nest at least three times a day, and if the bird was sitting on the nest every time I checked, to just leave it alone. If I found a nest without a bird, I needed to check to see if the eggs looked like they had been polished. If the eggs had any shine, then I needed to leave them alone. Jim told me that a fresh egg would look clean, but without a polished look. "There are no birds nesting now though," Jim said.

I asked Sam when we could go kite flying again. "Tomorrow," Sam said. "You have mastered flying a kite and helping me make abrasive line. Now, you have to learn how to make a kite." Sam told me it was not easy to make a good fighting kite, but in my mind, it looked simple. Sam gave me a skeleton of a kite he made, then he gave me two bamboo sticks and yarn. He told me to put it together like the one he had given me, and then he left. I put the kite together and felt that I did a good job. When Sam came back and looked at what I had done, he told me that if we put paper on my skeleton the kite would never fly. Sam took my work apart and showed me how to put it together. With Sam, everything had to be perfect. He showed me how to measure, and how to put on the strings. After many tries, he finally accepted my work.

Sam took me to a field where many young boys and adults from the better neighborhoods were flying kites. I brought my kite up to where the high flyers were. Then a man came up to Sam and told him he would not make money up here. He recognized our colors. Sam told the man that we were not there to wager. Instead, Sam was teaching me how to win in kite fighting. I stayed up there waiting for an opponent, and it took a while before a kite came close enough. Sam reminded me to make sure I attacked from above. When I finally got above my opponent, I dove down, caught the wind, made contact, gave line, and the other kite was gone. I won, but I was shaking from excitement.

Sam said, "Bring your kite up, there is another one ready to fight you." I said, "You take over, I am shaking and sick in the stomach." Sam told me I would feel better after I won the next battle. I was already above the other kite, I made a good dive down, made contact, and I won again. I felt a big rush going through my head. I was not scared anymore. The third fight I lost. Sam said, "Bring the line in fast." Sam inspected the line, cut the worn part off, and brought another kite up. We won three fights, then lost one. It was getting dark and it was time to quit. Before we left the field some of the people came over and shook hands with us and invited us back. There was such a difference when there was no wagering.

On the way home, I asked Sam why we left the kite in the air until somebody broke our line. Sam said, "It is for you to learn how to handle a kite and to learn to bring in the line fast." Then he added, "If we win all the time it is not exciting for our opponents." "But we are losing kites," I replied. Sam told me it was just a part of kite flying, and it would make me a better pilot. We went kite flying all through the season, and I learned a lot from Sam. We went to both the friendly and not so friendly places. At the end of kite-flying season we were well known among the kite-flying society. But Sam was not done with me, he wanted me to be able to build my own kite. No matter how many times I tried, Sam was never satisfied. Sam said, "Next kite-flying season, you have to make your own kite and abrasive line." Kite flying is one of my best memories from growing up.

I went to the pet store to check on the hatch box. The storeowner was not there, but the storekeeper said, "I have something to show you." He took me to the back and showed me four little pigeons. "Those came out of the hatch box," he said. I was very surprised, then I asked, "How do you feed them?" "We have our own formula," he said. He showed me something filled with ground-up corn. It looked like a sock with a little hole in it. I told him that after the rainy season I would find him the eggs they wanted. I told him the egrets would be nesting soon, and if they wanted those eggs, I could get them as many as they wanted. "No, thank you," he said.

Back in the village, I told Jim that the pigeon eggs I took to the pet store had hatched. Jim told me to go back in a week or so to see if the birds were still alive. "Why, they won't be alive?" I asked. Jim said, "It is very hard to raise new hatchlings, they need their mother's milk." "Birds don't have milk," I said. "It's not the milk you are thinking of," Jim said. "Birds produce milk in their craw, and if you can't imitate that, the young birds will die. That's why we who trap birds will never take the young birds out of a nest, until they start having feathers," he added. I went back to the pet store to check on the little birds, and to my surprise they had grown and looked very healthy. The storeowner told me they were very nice pigeons and gave me money. He told me he didn't want any egret eggs. I went back to Jim and told him that

The Excitement of Kite Combat | 57

the birds had grown and looked very healthy. Jim said, "Keep checking on them. If this experiment works, I will help you find the eggs the pet store wants after the rainy season."

At home, Sam told me that school would start soon, and he asked me to check on my school supplies. He helped me get it all together, then he said that I would have to study at least one hour a day. I did not like his idea. I liked to spend my vacation time with my friends. Sam said, "If you don't study, you might have to do this class over again, like last year's." In those days, if you didn't make the grade you would have to do the class over again with younger students, which was embarrassing. "But I was sick a lot," I said. "That is the reason to study," he said, "you will have some days next school year that you will be sick, too." As usual, I gave in to Sam's requests.

I knew that the rainy season was coming soon. The egrets were coming by the hundreds and starting to build nests in all the tall trees they could find. My native friends and I were sitting in front of Ming's store watching the egrets build their nests when Ming came out and asked us what we were watching. "Those noisy birds," I said. Ming said, "I would buy all the fresh egret eggs you boys can bring me." My native friends always let me do the talking. I told the boys we would go to Jim and ask how we could get the eggs. Jim told us if we wanted to harvest the eggs it was the time. He told us that after the birds were finished building their nests it would be harder to find fresh eggs. Then he told us it could be dangerous to climb the trees and if the police caught us, we would be locked up. "Not for taking the birds' eggs, but for climbing the trees," he added.

After we left Jim's house, we decided to give it a try anyway. I went to Ming and asked him for baskets and rope. Ming told me to find what we needed in the storeroom. We decided to hunt for eggs on a Saturday, early in the morning. I told Sam what our plan was and to wake me up before daylight. I had to promise Sam that I would not climb. If I did, he would tell my mother. The streets around the railroad station had big trees, and many side streets had big trees lining the roads. It was very early in the morning, and the streets were still. We lined the baskets with dry grass. Two of the boys began climbing, and three were handling the baskets. The harvest was so good that we lost track of time.

The next thing we knew, there were two policemen standing there. They told the boys to come out of the tree, then told me that we were being arrested and he had to take us to the police station. Somebody must have reported us. At the police station, they put all five of us in a cell. The policeman said, "We have to wait for the chief of police." We sat in the cell for what seemed to be a very long time without food or water. Then, a policeman came over and said the chief wanted to see me. I entered the chief's office and said to myself, "I know this man." I had seen him many times at our house, and on the tennis court, but never in uniform. He asked me if I knew why I was arrested. I said, "For taking egret eggs." The chief said, "First, climbing trees is dangerous. Second, the trees are government property. Third, I want to know who put you up to taking the egret eggs?" I said, "I did not know that climbing was against the law." The chief said, "Climbing is not against the law. Climbing trees that are government property is against the law." "Nobody put us up to taking the egret eggs," I said. I did not want Ming to get in trouble.

The two policemen came into the chief's office and

The Excitement of Kite Combat | 59

told the chief that the other boys did not know anything. They had all said I asked them to get the egret eggs. The police chief let us go and told us not to get arrested again, or he would lock us up for a long time. We had been at the police station all day. On our way out, the policemen were standing by the door and said, "Take the eggs with you, and don't let us catch you again." I took the eggs, but I did not want to bring them to Ming's store. I was afraid that the policemen would follow us. I told the boys that they did good by not telling. I told them we would bring the eggs to Jim. Jim said, "I already heard about the arrest, and I expected you would be locked up for a couple of days." "The boys did good, they all said that they were gathering eggs for me," I told him. I asked Jim if I could leave the eggs with him for the night. I told him I didn't trust the policemen, and I was worried they might have followed us. Jim told me it was okay, and he would take care of it.

When I got home, Sam asked me where I had been all day. I told Sam what happened and asked him not to tell anybody. Sam told me to go in the house for dinner. During dinner, my mother asked where I was all day. I told her that I was playing marbles with the boys down the street. My mother said, "From now on, when you leave the house, you'll tell me where you are going." This was hard for me, because I could not tell my mother where I was hanging out. I told Sam that I felt guilty not telling my mother the truth. Sam said, "Just tell me, and I'll cover for you." I took the eggs to Ming. He took the eggs, gave me money, and told me he was thankful that we did not mention his name to the police.

With the birds all having hatchlings at the same time, the rain, the wind, and the bird droppings created a stinky mess. It was funny to watch people on the street trying to protect themselves from it.

During the rainy season, we didn't have much to do, so we worked to sharpen our skills in the Indonesian martial art, Pentjak-Silat. I had been learning for about seven or eight years. Jim was our guru. Behind the chief's house was a building with only a roof, dirt floor and no walls. He held the village meetings there. The chief would watch our workouts sometimes. When Jim was at work and gone for days, the chief would take over the teaching.

The school bully picked on everybody. I was in a class behind him, and he never picked on me until I got in a fight with one of his friends and beat him. When word got around to him, he was waiting for me at the schoolyard before class. He told me if I ever picked a fight with one of his friends, I would have to deal with him. I told him that he was welcome anytime. He tried to slap me on the back of my head, but I was ready for him. Before he knew it, he was flat on his back. Class had started, so I walked away. He hollered that he was not done with me. After school, I was ready for a fight, but nothing happened. His group was standing together at the entrance of the schoolyard and I walked right by them.

At school the kids were talking about it. He said that he did not want to hurt me because he was a boxer. I said, "This is not a boxing match. It will be a street fight, and I will meet you anywhere anytime." More boys and girls were taking my side because nobody had ever stood up to him. The fight was going to be in the backyard of one of his friends. Many kids wanted to watch the fight. We faced each other; he was jumping around and saying to keep my fists up or he would blow my head off. His first blow busted my lip. I had blood all over my school clothes, but that was not the end of the fight. I kicked his feet out from under him and followed him to the ground. I put him in a very strong armlock. I was not about to break his arm, but I was hurting him. I asked him if he was giving up. He said, "Yes." I said, "Louder!" I wanted everybody to hear it, so I put more pressure on his arm until he said it loud enough. He said that I was not fighting fair. I told him he fights his way and I fight my way and if he wanted to do it all over again, I was willing. We never fought again, and he never bullied anybody anymore.

I told Jim about the fight at school. Jim said, "Now that everybody at your school knows that you can fight you have to avoid a fight as much as you can, and you have to work very hard on improving your fighting skills." At home, I asked Sam if he knew anything about Pentjak-Silat, but Sam said that he didn't. He also said, "But, when you get good at it, there are always people willing to find out how good you are." My mother asked me why my school uniform had blood on it. I told her that I had a fight at school, and I had to defend myself. She told me fighting would only cause trouble. At practice, I told Jim what Sam had said to me. Jim said, "That is why I have told you from the beginning that you should only work with the people you trust and never show others."

Jim told me on the other side of the village there was a man who was a master in Pentjak. He had a small tempeh factory. Jim told me that the only thing was that he wouldn't just teach anybody. He had picked two boys, twelve years of age or younger, to live with him and become masters when they were adults. He sent the kids to school; where we lived school was not free. He would never let them play with other kids. The boys helped him in the factory, did other chores, homework and then practiced their martial art. Their day started at 4:00 a.m. and was not over until nine or ten at night. I asked Jim how he knew so much about the master, and if he was a student of his. "No," Jim said, "Not of this man, there are many of these masters on the island, and some take as many as twelve boys. I was a failure after four years with my master. I asked him to be released because I had a girlfriend, and he let me go," he added. These boys would not mix with other people until they became masters themselves.

I asked Jim where the man lived. Jim said, "You can't miss it, it's the only white house with green windows and a picket fence." Then he told me he would never invite a stranger into his house. "I will find this man and become friends with him, too," I said. "Forget it," said Jim, "You are a white boy and he takes only the best young boys out of the village to become his followers." I found the house and remembered Jim saying to become a familiar face to win their trust. I found out that around four o'clock in the afternoon there was some shade on one side of the house and the boys would start practicing. After they were warmed up, the master would come out, give them instruction and then go back in the house. When he came out again, he tested the boys' work. Then they would all go in the house.

This went on for some time. Then one day after I saw the master go back in the house a voice next to me said, "Why are you always watching us?" It startled me, and I said, "I just saw you go back in the house. How is it possible that you are standing next to me?" He said, "I can do that. Now, tell me your story." I was lost for words. He said, "Don't be afraid." I told him I was amazed how skilled the young boys were and wondered how long it would take for an unskilled person to get that good. He said, "A lifetime, these boys have a contract with me, and will not leave me until they are masters and at least twenty-one years old." I said, "I hope you don't mind me watching you teaching the boys from the street." He said, "Yes, I do."

I was ready to leave and never come back when he told me to park my bicycle behind the house and come in. I couldn't believe what I heard. We were sitting in the front room and he offered me something to drink. Then, he asked me the real reason I had been watching them. I told him I wanted to learn from a real master. He asked how I knew that he was a real master. "Everybody in the village knows that," I said. "You hang out in the village?" he asked. "There are not many boys from your neighborhood that come to the village, and when they come, they always cause trouble," he added. "I am different," I said, "The village people are my friends." He said, "You must be the one who has done a lot of good for the village, and played soccer against your own team?" I said, "I did not play, the village boys did." He said, "I like that." Then, he asked me where I lived.

I told him, and then he told me that my cook was one of his tempeh customers. He asked me how old I was, and I told him I was eleven. "You are small for eleven," he said, "Most white boys your age are bigger." I told him I struggled with malaria, and the attacks from it held me back. He called the boys, they were older than me, to the front room, and they sat on the dirt floor. The master and I sat at the table and chairs. He told the boys that from now on I would be working out with them. He also told them not to work out outside with me. He told them to take me to the workout room to show me some basic moves. In the workout room were different kinds of weapons. The boys were very polite and shy, maybe because I was not one of them. I had a little experience in the fighting art, but it didn't take long for them to teach me the more advanced moves. I learned a lot working out with the boys. The boys were so fast, they seemed to know my next move before I made them. They were always very gentle with me, and they always worked to my speed. They seemed to like me, and after a workout they would always ask me to come back.

A malaria attack hit me, and I did not show up for some time. When I showed up again, the master called me to the front room and told me to sit on the chair. He said, "You must be serious about this, you can't come only when you feel like it." I said, "I am very serious, master, but I had a malaria attack and was too weak to work out." I think he felt sorry for me, and he asked me what kind of medicine I was taking for the malaria. "Quinine powder," I said. "That's the best medicine for it," he said, "but I will give you something to drink tomorrow. It will not cure the malaria, but it will give you more energy." Every day before practice I had to drink his medicine. It tasted much better than quinine.

The master told me that he and the boys would be gone for some time and his brother would be taking care of his business. I learned so much from this master and his boys, it gave me confidence. I practiced with them until my family and I had to move out of the area. The Japanese army kicked us out of our house, but that is for later in the story.

I went to Jim's house. He was home and invited me in. He said, "Sam must be really after you, making you do your schoolwork?" I said, "Not really, you have told me once not to tell anybody what we are doing. Now, I am asking you not to tell anybody what I am going to tell you." "What is the big secret?" Jim asked. "The great master has accepted me and told me not to tell anybody," I told him. Jim said, "That's impossible." "You know that I don't lie to you," I said. Jim said, "Do you know what you are getting into? When he takes you under his wings you have no life." He added, "I speak from experience." "I don't know what the great master's plans are. I don't live there," I said. "The great master expects me to work out with them every day. On weekends, I don't have to practice. He and the boys are on tour now. I don't know when they will be back. If you don't mind, I would like to work out with you again," I said. Jim said, "I still don't believe this." The boys asked where I had been all this time. I told them working on schoolwork and taking care of my animals. After practice, the boys said, "You must have practiced a lot at home?" "Yes, I have," I said.

Two more happy years went by. My friends and I, with the help from Jim, made lots of money doing business with Ming and the pet store. Sam and I grew very close. I was always looking forward to kite-flying time. I was able to make my own kites and abrasive line, but I never went kite flying without Sam. The great master became more of a father figure to me, and the boys and I became real good friends.

Things were changing at home; there must have been things that worried my mother, but she never showed it to me. Until one day when she told me that she had to let go of two of the servants. One was the man who took care of the animals, and she told me that she could no longer buy feed for all the animals. I asked, "What should I do with the animals?" "You have to get rid of them, sell them or give them away," she said. I told my mother that I would take care of the animals, and that there was still a lot of feed in storage.

I had to start my day at 4:00 a.m. so that I could be in school by 7:30 a.m. While I was in school, Sam fed the animals and gave them drinking water. After school, before I took care of the animals, Sam made me do my homework. After homework, it was back to the animals until about 6:30 p.m., but Sam let me work out with the great master and his boys. I told the master what was going on at my house. The great master said, "I'm convinced that you are serious about learning this martial art." Taking care of the animals and going to school was too much for me.

I went to the village and asked the chief if he could help me get rid of my animals. The chief said that he would talk to the people who went to the market to see if they could sell some of my animals. Then, the chief said, "Before you go, I want to tell you something. You know that there is a war going on?" I said, "Yes, my father has been gone for more than a year now." The chief said, "The bad thing is, the Dutch are losing, and you might never see your father again. The Japanese soldiers will be here soon, and I heard they are very brutal, they will take whatever they want."

I went to Jim; he was always teasing me. "What is going on now, you have a face like a horse," Jim said. I told Jim my story and told him that I was sad. He said, "You need help, I will talk to Ming. Then, the boys and I will sell as many animals as we can to him." I went to the pet store and asked them if they wanted to buy any of my animals. They did not. I said, "I have chickens that I have not seen anywhere else." "What kind are they?" he asked. "They are white chickens. Their feathers are so fine that it's like hair, they have blue legs, blue skin, and they lay green eggs." "Interesting," said the owner. "Bring some of their eggs and I will buy them from you." I brought him twelve eggs. He asked me how much money I wanted for them. I told him to hatch the eggs first to see if he liked the chickens.

One evening before dark, some village people came to my house and said that the chief had sent them. I said, "Yes, I'm expecting you." I showed them my animals. They all took some animals with them to sell on the market. The chickens, guinea hens, ducks, pigeons, rabbits and guinea pigs went fast. I always gave them a percentage. Some of the villagers would not take any money from me. They said that I was going through a bad time, and that they wanted to help. This went on for some time, and I was left with only the animals that did not sell right away. Jim and the boys sold many of my cage birds.

I had a big walk-in birdcage with many different birds. I opened the door to set them free, but it took a few days before they realized that they could fly away. Many stayed because they had babies, and others came back to roost depending on the food I put in the cage. I had two talking myna birds that I did not want to sell. These birds could speak whole sentences in Dutch or Indonesian. They could mimic the voice of a person so well that you couldn't tell the difference between the bird and the person. My myna birds needed special care. I gave one to the chief and one to Jim and asked them to take good care of them. The chief said, "These are the most expensive birds you have, and you are just giving them away?" I told him that I was giving them to him and Jim because I treasured their friendship.

The chief said it wouldn't be long before the Japanese

army would arrive. He told me the Dutch were on the run. I went to Jim and told him what the chief had said to me. Jim told me they would be here in one or two days. "What happens to the Dutch army?" I asked. Jim said, "Some went into hiding, but most of them were captured by the Japanese." "What will happen to the captured Dutch soldiers now?" I asked. He told me that they would become prisoners of war, but I did not understand what that meant.

At home, I asked Sam what could happen to us when the Japanese army arrived. Sam told me he didn't know, but he hoped they would leave us alone. That evening, just before dark, they came in big trucks, small trucks, motorcycles and wooden bicycles. We did not live on the main road, but they came in our neighborhood and stopped at different houses. We were one of the unfortunate ones. The Japanese soldiers came into our house and put all of us in one room. Then, they inspected all the rooms and looked around outside. The soldiers came back inside and picked on our oldest male servant. They spoke Japanese, but what they said nobody could understand.

We were all scared, so we went back to our quarters, turned all the outside lights off and used very little light in the house. It seemed that through the night there were people outside. The next morning, everything seemed to be all right, and nothing was missing. The servants told my mother that they would stay with us. A few days later, a jeep with four high-rank Japanese soldiers and an Indonesian interpreter came to the house. Through the Indonesian interpreter, the Japanese found out that my mother was the head of the household. The interpreter was polite, but he had to tell my mother what the Japanese wanted.

It was not good news. He told my mother that we had to move out and told us what we must leave behind. My mother said that she needed time to get everything packed and that she didn't know where to go. The interpreter talked to the Japanese to get us as much time as we needed. After they left, my mother told our servants that we had to move out because the Japanese were taking the house. The servants were very upset and wanted to know where we would move to. My mother told the servants that she did not know, but she must start looking. We started packing. We packed everything we could in bed sheets and anything that could hold stuff.

I went to the village to say goodbye to my friends. I went to the chief's house and told him what was going on. He said he already heard and wanted to know where I was going to live. I told him I did not know, but that my mother was looking. The chief asked when he would see me again. I told him as soon as we were settled in the new place. The chief gave me the money box, just in case. I went to Jim's house, but he was not home. I knew that my master and the boys were not home. My young friends were as unhappy as I was. I told them that I would be back as soon as I was settled at the other place, but I wanted them to continue with our dream of a fish farm. I said, "I don't know how much money we already have. I have never counted it, but it seems that we have lots of money, and I'm sure that the chief and Jim will help you." The boys told me it wouldn't be the same without me.

My mother found a place, and we children – my sister, my two younger brothers and I – were ready to move. My mother gave the servants lots of stuff. Among other things, Sam got my father's bicycle. After everything was loaded in the horse-drawn carriages the servants said goodbye to us. I walked to the end of our property with Sam. He looked at me and said, "You will become a good person, you have a strong will. Be polite and stick to your studies." He rode off on the bicycle and I never saw Sam again.

Two female servants stayed with us. My mother told them that she could not pay them anymore. I don't know how my mother found the place. We left early in the morning, and it took us all day to get to our new place. It was a very small house and there was already a family living in there, a mother and her two sons. After everything was unloaded and the drivers had been paid, it was almost midnight. That night we slept on the floor. The next morning, when we started to unpack, I was shocked at how small the house was, but it had a big fenced-in back yard. At breakfast, my mother told me that we must make the best of our situation because we would be living there for a long time. Those years had been the best years of my life. The sad thing is that I never saw the chief, Jim, or my young friends again, but I will live with the memories forever.

THE JAPANESE OCCUPATION (1942-1945)

OUR NEW SITUATION WAS very disappointing, and I was angry. I had lived in a big house with many servants. I had been treated like a prince in the village. Now, I had to start all over. I inspected the fence because I still had some leftover animals that I took with me. It looked good, and there was a gate that led to the farmer's fields. My animals hadn't been fed since the day before. I took the chickens, goat and sheep out of their crates and let them free in the back yard. I put the pigeons in a bigger crate but kept them locked up. I fed the chickens and pigeons and gave them water. Then, I had to find grass and brush for my goat and sheep. After I fed and watered them, I went in the house for lunch and to meet the other family.

The family was friendly, and my mother got along fine with them. They had two dogs, a big German Shepherd and a small dog. The German Shepherd was very aggressive and didn't like my animals. The next morning, I saw goats and sheep tied on ropes in the fields behind the house. I took my animals and tied them in the field away from the other animals. A group of native kids came over and told me that the place was taken. I had no choice but to take the animals home. I had to feed them, so I took my grass-cutting tool and basket to cut grass. Everywhere I tried to cut grass the native kids kept telling me that the place was taken. I knew that they didn't want a white kid cutting into their territory. I kept walking until the boys didn't follow me anymore.

In the distance, I saw a tobacco plantation. The tobacco plants were almost ready for harvest. There was a lot of security, and no trespassing signs everywhere. I went in and started cutting grass. It did not take long before a white man approached me and asked me why I was cutting grass where it was not allowed. I told him that the Japanese soldiers took our house and we just moved here. I explained that we didn't have any servants anymore, and that I was trying to cut grass in the fields closer to home, but a group of native boys wouldn't let me. He said, "Those boys don't own the fields." Then, he asked me how many animals I had. I said, "I have two sheep and a goat, and I have to find grass for them every day."

He said, "If you promise me that your animals will not run loose, and you keep them out of the way. I will tell my foreman to keep an eye on them too, and you can cut grass here." The Indonesian foreman came and told me where I could tie my animals and cut grass. I told the foreman that I really appreciated what they were doing for me. I took my animals through another route to the tobacco plantation to avoid the native boys. After the tobacco was harvested, the villagers had permission to cut grass and graze their animals on company grounds. The group of native boys who gave me trouble before were at it again. I was cutting grass and one of the boys started cutting grass very close to me. I told him, "Get lost, this patch is mine," and the whole group came over. The white man and the foreman came to my rescue. The white man told the boys to leave me alone and that I could cut grass anywhere I wanted.

I got to know the neighbor boy; he was the son of our landlord. His father owned the house we lived in, four other houses, and all the fields behind the houses. His name was Norman and we became friends. Norman's house had a big yard with lots of fruit trees. They also had horses and carriages that they used as taxis. Norman had an Indonesian mother. I invited Norman to look at my animals. He said that I took good care of my animals and he really liked the pigeons. I told him that he could have some of them, but he refused. I told him that I had a hard time finding food for my sheep and goat. Norman said, "All the fields behind the houses all the way to the tobacco plantation are my mothers." I told him that there was a group of boys who were cutting grass and let their animals graze on those same fields, and that they had been giving me a hard time when I tried. Norman said he would go with me the next time I went to cut grass. Norman knew all the boys by name, and he told them that I could cut grass and let my animals graze on his property. I still made sure to stay out of their way.

One evening, there was Gamelan music coming from the village, and I instantly knew what it was. The village people were having a contest in their Pentjak skill. I had been through this with my master and his students many, many times, but I had never seen a real contest. Norman came over and invited me to go with him to the village to watch the fights. The fights were mainly young boys and men with their Gurus on the sidelines. The fighters were dressed in their fighting clothes: a headdress, bare upper body, a sarong around their waist, shorts, and bare feet. A fighter stepped in the ring, which was a circle drawn on a cleared piece of ground, and did his kata while the music played soft and slow. When the other fighter stepped in the ring the music got louder and faster. If the first fighter did not want to fight the challenger, then he stepped out of the ring. The music would slow down again until there was a fight. As the fight got more intense the music would become louder and faster. When one fighter had enough, he would step out of the ring, but if the person was in a painful hold, he would tell the other fighter he gave up. Most of the fights did not last long. It was more of a friendly contest.

While Norman and I watched the fights, I heard some of the village people saying, "This white boy is out of place here." Then a boy stepped in the ring, and there was no challenger. The music slowed down. If no one came forward the fights would be over, and he would be the champion. I remembered him as the boy who gave me the most trouble in the fields. I stepped in and did my kata. He stepped out to talk to his teacher. Norman tried to talk me out of it; he told me I would be killed because the boy was so good. I told Norman that I knew what I was doing.

The boy stepped back in the ring. I heard people shouting from the sidelines. They said it was time to teach the white boy a lesson. The boy made all kinds of fake attacks. I stood with my arms to my side watching every move he made. In my head I heard my Master telling me to be ready and make it as short as possible. He attacked, but I was ready. I blocked him, then let him have it. He was bleeding out of his mouth. That made him really angry and he came at me with all he had. I was ready, and

I let him have it again. This time I dropped him hard to the ground, but I did not finish him. I gave him time to get up again, and I knew I had the upper hand. I wanted him to tell me that he had enough, but he attacked again, and I floored him. I waited for him to get up again. I wanted to teach him a lesson. He got up and wanted to attack again, but he was in no condition to fight. His teacher stepped in and stopped the fight. I asked Norman to get me out of there as fast as he could. "Follow me," he said, "I know my way around here." Norman wanted to know where I learned to fight. "I'll tell you tomorrow, take me home first!" I said.

The next day, Norman followed me everywhere I went. He wanted to know who taught me the fighting skills. I made him promise not to tell anybody. I told him my father did, but he was not here to teach me anymore. I became Norman's hero, and he would tell anybody about the fight. Norman became my shadow. The word got around in the village that a white boy had beaten their champion. When I went to the village to watch the people practice their martial art, some of the older teachers politely asked me to work out with them. There were no masters in this village; everybody was learning from each other. I practiced with the village, and I had no problem with the boys my age, not even in the fields. The boy I beat stayed away from me. I put my animals at the best grazing spots and cut grass at the best places too.

Norman kept bugging me to teach him how to fight. I showed him the very basic moves and told him to practice in front of a big mirror and when he thought he had mastered it, he could try it on me. Every time Norman tried his skills on me, I would tell him that he was not fast enough and had to practice more.

I wanted to know the village people better. When I walked through the village, people greeted me with the word "sinjo." It was a polite way of addressing a white boy. The older men sometimes asked me to come in their house and have tea with them. I had lots of questions, but the conversations always came down to my fighting skills. I always told them my father taught me. I told Norman that I wanted to be friends with the village people, but they wouldn't open up to me. Norman said, "You don't need to be friends with them, they are low-class people." I felt insulted since this was coming from Norman, and he had an Indonesian mother.

All the Dutch nationals had to register. The Japanese put some families in internment camps. Many families were split up: boys twelve years and up went to the men's camp, girls and the younger children went to women's camp. Some families didn't have to go to camp, and we were one of them. I don't know if we were the "lucky ones." With many families put into camps, more and more families had to move in together for safety and economic reasons. Living outside with no income made life hard. Our two female servants stayed with us. They helped my mother immensely with income and getting food.

Every day there were bargain hunters going house to house asking the ladies if they had something for sale. For most families that was their only income. When my mother had something of value to sell, a servant would sell it in town for more money. Down the road from us, the Japanese used a school as a military camp. In front of the camp was a guardhouse with a Japanese soldier on guard at all times. Anybody going by the guardhouse had to stop and bow to the soldier, and if you didn't you got punished. One day my mother walked by the guardhouse and said, "Today it is my turn, and tomorrow it will be yours." The Japanese soldier answered in Dutch, "I don't stand here for my pleasure." My mother never went by that guardhouse again.

With most leading Dutch people in internment camp, things were falling apart. Everything was run by the Japanese military. When they needed workers, they just picked anybody off the street for whatever was needed. This news traveled fast through the villages. When the truck came to pick people up there was nobody to be found. That made the soldiers angry. They took it out on the chiefs and the women who were left in the village. They beat them up and went into their houses and broke a lot of things. Then, they told the chiefs to have workers ready by 6:00 a.m., otherwise the punishment would be severe. After this incident, many people volunteered, including me, to avoid harassment.

There were not many men left in the village to do their own chores. Boys as young as twelve years were picked up to work for the Japanese soldiers. When I was done with my animals I would go to the village and help the women take care of their animals. I asked Norman if he could help me take the village animals to the fields so they could graze. Norman did not say anything; he just shook his head. He must have thought that I was crazy, but he never did not help. I said to Norman, "You know where to find me, if needed." Norman always helped me with my animals without me asking for it.

The men in the village were thankful for what I was doing. They told me that the soldiers worked them very hard. They organized so that some of them could stay in the village to take care of the animals and other things. When the Japanese soldiers found out, they came back to beat the men with a cane and made them come to work. The soldiers needed more workers, so they started picking up us men and boys who were not in internment camp. Most of these people had never done labor work. They had a very hard time. We did not work in big groups. The soldiers divided us in crews of six, and one of us was the foreman. The foreman had to make sure that his crew worked to the satisfaction of the Japanese. If not, he would be punished.

The first job I got was weeding rice fields. There was a water plant choking off the young rice plants. The work was very simple. You would stand ankle to knee deep in the mud, pull the weeds out, and put them on the narrow walkways between the fields. I was put to work with a crew of whites who had never done this kind of work. It was a disaster. The soldiers were constantly barking at our crew, and some of us got stroked with a cane. To top it off, there were leeches in the water. When a leech attached itself to your hands or legs it would grow from a real tiny thing to as big as a finger in a hurry. Some of my crew-members just took the beatings; they refused to go back in the field. The soldiers put sawed-off fifty-gallon drums of warm saltwater on the walkways. The saltwater took the leeches off in no time, but the water became a slimy bloody mess. The Japanese gave us soap and clean water to wash ourselves off.

The tobacco fields were ready for replanting. There were hundreds of workers in the fields, all divided in groups of six. Some of the groups were for planting, and some were for putting up shade for the young plants against the afternoon sun. The shade was made from banana trees. A banana tree would peel like an onion, so it was easy to make a shade out of it for the young plants. Then, there was the watering crew, where I was put to work. I didn't know where all these people were coming from; they were all strangers to me. I didn't know one person on my crew, and I think the Japanese did that on purpose. We were given a yoke, two five-gallon cans and a small scoop. There was a small path going down to the river. The first trips went okay, but after a few trips the spilled water made it slippery, so we had to be very careful going uphill. If you fell and spilled all your water you would get punished, usually strokes with a cane.

We also had water trucks in the fields. The crews working the water trucks got to work on flat ground, but they had more ground to cover. The dead plants were replaced, and the watering went on until the soldiers were sure that all the young tobacco plants made it. The first few days my neck and shoulders were very sore, and I got a painful sunburn. I was not wearing a shirt or shoes anymore, so my feet were also a little tender.

Back at home I now had five sheep and three goats to care for, and I had difficulty making time for it. I asked Norman if he could sell the animals for me. He said he would try, and that he would take care of them until he had them sold. When Norman gave me the money for the animals he had sold I asked how much I owed him, but he told me I didn't owe him anything. I gave the money to my mother.

Another job I did for the Japanese was harvesting coconuts. Again, there were multiple jobs the soldiers made us do. First, there were climbers. Then, the group who took the husk off the nut. Another group who broke the nut open and took the meat out of it. Then, the group who took the meat to the dry floor and spread it out to dry in the sun. I was a climber, and coconut trees were very tiring to climb. The coconut trees we climbed had notches cut in the trunk that we used as steps. The tall trees swayed a lot in the wind. We also carried a sickle up the tree. I didn't know how many years it took before the nuts could be harvested. It was very difficult to get up to the crown of the tree. You didn't have branches or anything to hang onto, so you had to hug the main trunk with one arm and start cutting the coconuts off until you cut a hole through the nuts and could climb up to the crown.

If you could get through the hole and up to the crown without being bitten or stung by the critters that lived there, you were lucky. The most common critters in the coconut trees were snakes, squirrels, scorpions, centipedes, spiders and the occasional coconut crab. The snakes and squirrels always tried to get away from you. The other critters were the ones to watch out for. I found out when I stayed on the green part of the crown, I had less chance of being bitten or stung. After climbing, we always had cuts, scrapes, bruises, tree rash on our chest, and sometimes red spots and swelling. We knew we got bit or stung but never felt it.

The trees were so tall that if you fell out you would die. I had only one incident where I almost fell out of a tree. After I cut all the ripe coconuts off the tree, I had to cut all the brown stuff off too. I had the tree cleaned and was climbing down the tree. I had one arm around the main trunk and brought my other hand around the backside of the trunk when I felt an awful pain through my hand and arm. I looked at my hand and saw that I had flattened two scorpions. I scraped them off and came down the tree as fast as I could. On the ground I went down on my knees and cried. The foreman knew right away what happened. These scorpions were small, brown and almost transparent. There was no medicine and the pain was unbearable. They made a concoction from some leaves and vinegar. By the time I got home my arm was swollen, I felt sick and my heart was throbbing in my throat. Even with the help from the village medicine man, it took some time before I got full use of my arm. For a hungry twelve-year-old it was hard work.

Things began to ease up a little because the Japanese found workers from other places. They also put prisoners to work, and the prisoners did most of the dirty work. They were treated worse than we were. I helped the villagers with their animals and with harvesting their crops. The village boys and I got along better now, but it was never like the other village where we were as close as brothers. These new-found friends always made a contest out of everything we did, but Sam and Jim had me well prepared for this. I had to prove myself every time.

The first time we went to catch fish by hand the boys put their catch all in one basket, but they did not want mine. After they found out how well I could catch fish and shrimp, they changed their minds. We put our catch together and divided the catch equally. We also gathered termites, the flying kind. When they came out, they always flew toward light, so we waited under a street light and gathered as many as we could. Then, we would fry them. We also went after crickets and other bugs. There was one kind of cricket, that we called mole crickets. These critters liked dry ground, and they would leave little mounds. In August and September, we could find two in each hole. We took special care when digging them up so we wouldn't crush them because they were tasty when fried.

We also found the beetle grubs that lived in old rotten

palm trees. When we found such a tree, we would split it open and gather many grubs. The rotan grub was hard to get. They were small, but they got special treatment from the village people. For every grub we needed a ripe coconut. There are three soft spots in a coconut, and we would open one, pour the water out, put the little grub in the coconut, and close the holes. Then, we would put the coconut in a holder with the holes facing up. When we opened the coconut the grub inside had grown many times in size. It was all coconut meat. We would heat up a pan without oil, throw the grub in the pan, and cover it. We would wait for the grub to explode, turn it over, take the head off and let it cook. When it was done it looked like a fried egg, but it was very rich.

It was always fun harvesting fruit with the villagers. We would climb the trees and pick the fruit by hand. To get the ones on the outer branches we would use a bamboo pole with a basket at the end. There were many trees with ants living in them. There were two main types of ants: the big orange and green ones that were very aggressive, and the little black ones. We would cover our body with wood ashes before we tried to climb the trees. First, we tried it on the big ants. We would climb up the tree, but we would have to come down in a hurry, and by the time we got down we always had painful welts all over us. The little black monsters let us climb a little higher up the tree, but besides biting they would secrete acid in your face that would make it so you couldn't keep your eyes open. We washed our eyes out with water, but we would still end up with red burning eyes. The boys started shooting the ripe fruit out of the trees with a slingshot. The trick was not to hit the fruit, but the stem, so that the other boys could stand under the tree and catch the falling fruit. I was a catcher, but it was no fun standing under a tree with ants falling on you and biting you.

I asked the boys if I could be one of the shooters. The boy who fought me said only the best shooters will shoot. I said, "Let's find out who are the best shooters." These boys had never seen me handle a slingshot, and I was very good. I put a marble on a fence post, walked back a certain distance and told them we would all have ten shots at it. The ones who could hit the marble would be the shooters. They wanted me to shoot first. I hit the marble three times out of my ten shots. None of the boys hit the marble once. Again, I gained a little more respect from them.

It was time for me to work for the Japanese again. This time it was harvesting hot peppers. The fields were full of so many ripe hot peppers that the air even smelled hot. The group I worked with were all native kids that I didn't know. We had to fill baskets lined with banana leaves. I thought this was pretty easy. After picking for a while I had to pee, but my fingers were burning. I did not think about it and I touched my jewel. It burned for the rest of the day! Then, I saw three boys carrying two baskets in between them. I thought I could carry my own basket, which was my second mistake. I carried the basket on my back, and by the time I got to the truck the juice of the ripe hot peppers had dripped down my back all the way down to the cheeks of my butt, which was so painful! After work, I went to the river and sat in the water for hours.

The next day, I did it the way the other boys did. I learned that when we had to pee, we would just pee in our pants. Peeing in our pants was not the worst part of the job. We also had to deal with the little bugs that would bite us in the face, mosquitoes that would bite us anywhere they could, and ants that would attack our feet and legs. After work, we would go to the river to clean up and soak our hands. Most of the jobs for the Japanese didn't last very long, anywhere from one day to one week. This gave me time to spend with Norman and the boys from the village.

For protection, the villagers built little guardhouses by the entrances to the villages. After dark, there was always somebody in the guardhouse. They would communicate by pounding on hollowed-out bamboo. Sometimes I visited the men in the guardhouse and asked them many questions. We started talking about the Japanese soldiers. The village men were very unhappy with them. This was one of the reasons they built the guardhouses. When the drunken Japanese soldiers were walking down the street, they would always make trouble, and if you resisted them, they could kill you on the spot. The soldiers would go into the houses in the village looking for women. After my conversations I understood why our servants knew when to hide the women of the house.

More and more white families were moving in together deeper into the villages. The families were very poor. I got to know a white mother and her four blond boys who lived in the village. They were very poor. My mother always fed these boys when we had food. Their ages were between fifteen and nine. Sometimes the boys would come play with Norman and me at my house. We didn't have electronic toys or games at the time. We entertained ourselves with other games and made our own toys. There was a big citrus fruit with a very thick shell. This shell became our material for building toys. We carved all kinds of things from it: cars, trucks, horse- or ox-drawn carriages. When we could find enough material, we would build cities, farms, train stations and other things. The oldest boy was very good at carving, and the only tool he had was his pocketknife. We spent whole days on these projects, just for them to be thrown away the next day because the citrus peel had wilted.

Playing marbles was another game we spent a lot of time on. Knife throwing was also a big contest for us. We used a banana stem for a target. The throwing knives were specially made, but they were easy to come by in the village. Sometimes the villagers had a knife-throwing tournament with prizes. The villagers set up a real target made of soft wood. Every contestant brought his own knives. Every contestant got three tries with two knives. The person with the most points was the winner. Most of the time, first-place prize was throwing knives. Again, the oldest of the four brothers was very good at this.

The four brothers liked to spend time with Norman and me. They also liked to read. Norman's father had many interesting and educational books. When these boys got ahold of interesting books, they would lose track of time. They had to be home before dark, because the three oldest were night blind. When they stayed too long and had to go home in the dark, they would form a line with the youngest up front and the oldest in back, all holding onto one another. It was hard for the youngest boy because the village kids were always teasing them. Sometimes, Norman and I would follow them at a distance to make sure that they were not teased and could get home safely.

One day, when we were catching fish by hand, the Japanese soldiers were watching us pull our traps out. Then, one of the men told us not to pull all the traps because the Japanese had a habit of taking whatever they wanted. We only filled one basket to take to the market. It was my turn to work for the Japanese again. They loaded all the workers on the trucks but left two crews of twelve men behind. I was one of them. The Japanese needed us to catch fish for them. I did not see anything to catch fish with. They made us carry big baskets that water could flow through. The baskets had a narrow neck with a strap to carry it over the shoulder. The Japanese soldiers carried backpacks. When we got to the river the Japanese threw explosives in the deep water and lots of fish and other critters came floating to the surface. It was our job to collect them. If a fish slipped through and floated downstream the Japanese would get really upset and start screaming at us. We caught so many fish and critters that we could not carry the load. A truck had to come down to haul the load. I only went one time but the Japanese kept doing this until there was hardly any life left in the river. It was very hard on the village people who depended on the river.

I was with a crew weeding sweet potato fields. I had to pull the weeds by hand. I had to save the grass and put the weeds in a specially made basket. The Japanese didn't want us to carry any tools because they wanted to make sure that we would not dig the sweet potatoes out. The sweet potatoes were growing on raised beds. I found one potato sticking out of the ground. I pulled it out and ate it. Somehow a Japanese soldier saw it, and he called me to the narrow path between the fields. He made me stand at attention, then he kicked me in the shin with his military boots. When I bent over, he hit me on the nose and gave me a bloody nose. Then, he kicked me on my anklebone, which hurt the most. This went on until I could not stand up anymore. I was in pain for some time, but everything healed except a little puncture wound under my anklebone. My ankle stayed swollen and was very painful.

Then, a stinky fluid came out of the wound and flies were always trying to get to it. At night, my mother gave me a towel to wrap my foot in to keep the bed clean. We had no medicine. The village people tried their medicine, but it did not help.

I was put to work at a brick factory loading trucks. The loading ramp was very primitive: it was just a pit dug in the ground to make the truck bed the same height as the ground we were standing on. We were divided into three groups: loaders, stackers and carriers. I was a carrier. They gave me a yoke and two baskets to carry the bricks. We carried the bricks straight from the oven to the truck. I could not keep up with the crew because of my ankle injury, and the Japanese kept yelling and hitting me on the legs. Lucky for me, my crew foreman could speak Japanese; by now many Indonesians could speak Japanese. He told the Japanese men in charge that I had a bad leg. The Japanese soldiers looked at my wound, and then told me to get lost. I took a short-cut through a village and sat down in a shady place across from a barbershop. Flies were bugging me, so I picked a twig off a plant with some leaves on it to keep the flies off my foot.

I did not notice that somebody was watching me. He came to me and asked why I was crying. I told him that I was supposed to be working at the brick factory, but my foot hurt so much that I could not keep up, so the Japanese soldiers told me to leave. The man told me his name was Jasman, and I came to know him as Max. He told me he lived across the street and invited me to come with him. I did not want to go in his house. Max asked why I was hesitant to come in. I told him that the stuff coming out of my wound would smell up his house. "You have to come in and let me take care of your wound," he said. I sat on a chair with my foot on a newspaper. Max called his wife to look at my wound. His wife looked at it and said we needed to take care of it right away. His wife's name was Siti, and I called her Sara. Sara said if we waited any longer, I could get blood poisoning. I told them I had no medicine available at home. Sara told me to sit on the chair and wait while she boiled some herbs to clean the wound.

While she was working on the concoction for my foot, she gave me food, and it was very tasty. After I finished my meal, she asked me if I wanted more. I could have eaten more, but I said no. Sara put a steaming bowl by my foot and told me to put my foot in it. "It's very warm, keep your foot in it for as long as you can stand it," Sara said. Then, she put a towel over my foot to keep the steam in. It was so painful that I had to use all my inner strength that I had learned in martial arts not to scream. After the water cooled down, Sara put the towel on the floor and told me to put my foot on it. This made a lot of stuff came out of the wound, but she told me it still needed a lot more care. Sara cleaned the wound one last time and put some brown liquid around it. They told me to come back the next day. This went on for some time and Sara always fed me, which was the best part of the treatment. The swelling went down, and my foot and I felt so much better, but Sara insisted on checking my wound daily. I had no objections because there was always food. There was no more stuff coming out of the small hole in my foot. Max gave me yellow powder to put on the wound that would keep the flies away. My wound healed, and finally I could run again.

I told Max and Sara that I could never repay them for what they had done for me. Sara said, "Yes, you can. Just come by every day." I left with tears in my eyes. A few days went by before I realized how much this Indonesian couple meant to me. Max and Sara were happy to see me again and invited me to come in. We sat at the table and Sara put some snacks out and told me not to hold back. Max noticed that I was a little withdrawn. He said, "I know what is wrong with you; you feel bad that you can't repay us." He added, "The tables are turned now, and you have become a have-not. We are glad to help, so what is wrong with that? Besides, we have no children and we love you."

Max said, "Let me tell you my story. I'm the youngest of six siblings, and my mother found work with a Dutch couple fresh out of Holland. These people could not speak a word of Indonesian, but my mother spoke a little Dutch. My mother was pregnant with me. When it was time to give birth, her master insisted that I be born in a hospital. My mother insisted that village people don't give birth in hospitals, but I was born in the hospital. From then on, this couple took care of me and spoiled me. By the time, I was two years old I did not want to go home to the village with my mother. When my mother told the Dutch couple this, they asked for permission to raise me as their own. My parents thought I would be better off, so I grew up with the Dutch family. I spoke only Dutch to my adopted parents and Indonesian to my mother. I did not have much contact with my father or the other siblings, but I was with my mother every day."

Max continued, "When it was time for me to go to school my adopted parents wanted me to go to Dutch school, but they could not get me in under my own name. So, my stepfather, the only father I had known, gave me his name. I blended well with the Eurasians and the Indos. To please my parents, I did my best, and stayed in the top five all through high school. My white parents went back to Holland because there was a war in Europe. I chose to stay in Indonesia. My adopted parents left me well taken care of."

Now I understood why Max and Sara had such a fancy house in the village. The house was built with good timber and bamboo, it had a dirt floor, a tile roof, a big front room, a barber shop, a dining room, two meeting rooms, four bedrooms, a big kitchen, electricity, running water, and a bathroom and toilet.

Sara had her own business. She made snacks to sell to the public. Early in the morning, the street vendors would come to Sara's kitchen and pick up the snacks. Then, the vendors would go house to house to sell the snacks. Late in the afternoon, they came back to Sara and she would meet with them in the small meeting room in the kitchen. Sara would count the money and give them a percentage. Sara told me that she no longer could do business. The ingredients were expensive and hard to come by, and people no longer had any money to spend.

Max held meetings at his house, and sometimes the meetings would last for days. I didn't know where these men came from. I spent time with Sara in the kitchen. Sara would be busy cooking, making snacks, coffee and refreshments for the men. I enjoyed helping Sara and her two helpers with the cooking. Sara always tried to teach me how to cook, and if I was smart, I could have been a good cook, but I was more interested in eating.

Max introduced me to a boy across the street from them; his name was David. David was Indo; he had a Dutch father and an Indonesian mother. His stepfather was a Chinese businessman who owned stores, fish farms, and a brick factory. Max told me that David was a very smart boy, and he could speak four languages. When the

Dutch schools were closed, David went to Chinese school where they also had to learn Japanese. David's mother made sure that David spent most of his time studying. Sometimes he could play outside on their property with the native kids. When I came to his place his mother always made us go in the house and play, and she was always close by. She didn't want me to talk about the hardship of the Indos. One day, she asked me not to play with David anymore. She told me that David had too many questions. I respected her wishes.

I went back to work for the Japanese, this time on a road gang. My job, along with many other people, was to make gravel. They would bring us to a pile of rocks, and we made gravel out of it. We had no tools, and no eye protection. We smashed the rocks against each other, put the small pieces in a basket to be graded, then carried them to where they would be boiled into tar. I could not see how the road was repaired. I had to keep busy making gravel. The Japanese soldiers and foreman made sure that we kept working, and they were very willing to use their bamboo canes on us. At the end of the workday, many people had bloody and smashed fingers.

Next, I was put to work planting castor beans. We had to plant the beans alongside the road and in people's yards, but nobody ever complained. The Japanese were almighty. Planting castor beans must have been going on for some time because we also had to harvest the beans. I was told that the plant and beans were poisonous, but the natives told me that the milky pitch could cure toothaches. I had proof of that. I had a cavity in my tooth that was very painful. One of the older workers in my gang told me to be very careful with it because if I got the pitch on a healthy tooth it would break into pieces. I asked him if he could help me. He told me to open my mouth and then told me that he saw a big hole in my tooth. He took the spine of a coconut leaf, put castor bean pitch on it, and put it in my tooth. It tasted bitter, but in an instant the pain was gone. It was a luxury to have a toothbrush back then. After a few treatments, the tooth turned black. Then, it took some time before I lost my tooth. No more toothache.

Taking care of horses for the Japanese was my easiest job. Our jobs were cleaning the stalls, feeding, walking, brushing and taking the horses to the river for a bath. We were permitted to ride the horses, but we had no saddles or blankets to put on their backs. It was okay for a while, but then we got very painful boils on our behinds. I went to Max and Sara because I knew they had medicine. Sara looked at the boils and said it was from horsehair and horse sweat. "Stay off the horses," she said. I could hardly walk.

The Japanese got meaner by the day. I could not figure out why because all the workers did their best, but it was never good enough. The Japanese always found some excuse to beat the workers. I never got paid for the slave work I did. Sometimes, I would get coupons for rice, sugar, beans, salt and other things. When I got a coupon for meat – horse, buffalo or other kinds – I would stand in line at 3:00 a.m. but when it came to my turn they had always run out. I told Max my frustration about not being able to cash out my coupons. Max told me the system was very corrupt, but that I could give him my expired coupons and then pick the stuff up at his place. I got enough stuff that I could share some with the very needy Indos in the village.

Before I met Max and Sara, I kept an eye on Chinese funerals. The very rich had elaborate ways to pay their last respects. The casket was put in a horse-drawn hearse with glass side panels. Walking behind the hearse were the mourners all dressed in white, then people walking in their best clothes, and behind them were the relatives in horse-drawn carriages. At the cemetery they went through their ceremonies. The graves were elaborately designed out of marble and had canopies. They would leave a lot of offerings at the grave: food, fruit and some valuables. I asked the natives why nobody ever stole the offerings. The natives were very superstitious, and they believed that when you took that stuff you would get sick and die, or you would lose your mind. I waited until after dark before I went back. The cemetery was very big, and it was so dark that I could not see very far in front of me. I had trouble finding the grave with the offerings. When, I finally found it, the birds, rats and other animals had already sampled the food. I took what was left, sorted it out under a street light, and shared it with other Eurasians in the village. They never asked where I got it. There were little statues and other valuables. I always brought those back on the next trip.

ENTERTAINMENT THE NATIVES ENJOYED

THE NATIVES ENJOYED MARTIAL arts, empty handed or stick fighting. They enjoyed watching cockfights and bull fights. Bull fighting was bull against bull, and it was very dangerous because the bulls were huge. Racing bulls were slender. Bull racing involved two bulls that were held together with a yoke and a ladder fastened to the yoke. A man would stand on the ladder holding onto ropes. To keep the bulls running in a straight line he would use a whip;, there were many accidents.

After the crops were harvested it was time for cricket fights. Almost everybody was into this, even the young boys. These crickets were either black or brown with a yellow stripe on the wings behind their neck. This was a serious pastime for the adults. The crickets fought in a wooden box with a rough bottom that was about five inches by eight inches. It had glass sides that were about four inches high, and a wooden partition in the middle. When people would find crickets that were about the same size the owners would agree to fight them, and then they would put the crickets on each side of the partition. Then they would twirl some corn hair tied to the spine of a coconut leaf. This would make the cricket so angry it would attack anything. The partition was pulled up and the crickets would fight. Most of the fights didn't last long because the loser would run, and it was over. These fights would go on all day.

In late afternoon, on special occasions, the women would bring big plates woven out of bamboo lined with banana leaves with lots of food on them. There would be rice in the middle, greens, meat, fresh fish, dried salted fish, and chicken all around it. The men would eat with their hands, all out of the same plate. A small bowl with water was placed next to each man where they could put their fingers, so the rice would not stick to them. After the big meal, they would face to the east, get down on their knees and pray. This was the time I disappeared. The Indonesians believed that the graves on the hill were holy and the crickets were the spirits of those men.

When I heard the story, I asked the master cricket fighter if it was true. He said, "You see that man standing there, smoking a cigarette?" I said, "Yes, he is strange." "I'll tell you what happened to him," the master said. "When he was your age, he was the most daring kid in the village. He tried to catch a holy spirit from the hill. He went up there but did not come back. We found him back in another village. Nobody knew him there, and he did not know where he was. He was filthy. He had not taken a bath for a long time. According to our medicine man, the spirit had taken his mind. We had to tie him up to give him a bath. We also had to tie him up when he got his angry attacks," he explained. "He is better now, thanks to our medicine man," he added.

There was another cricket contest coming to the village. The villagers went in the fields at night to find the best crickets. I visited the top master and watched him work his crickets. It was such a big event for the villagers. The man said, "I have good crickets, but the men who are coming have been champions for many seasons." I went to the hill with the holy graves to investigate. I had dug up mole crickets on this hill. I had learned a lot from Jim, and I remembered the scorpions, and why the critters on the hill were bigger and stronger. I was looking for signs of where the crickets might be hiding. I felt like Jim was there with me, teaching me what to look for. I found a clean hole next to a rock ledge with what looked like cricket droppings. It was very quiet on the hill, and kind of scary, and I began to think about how I would have to come back after dark. I had a flashlight, but I didn't use it much because batteries were very hard to get. I got the cricket. It was a beautiful big brown one with strong legs, big jaws, and long antennas. I kept him in a box at home, and I was wondering if there were any ill effects for taking the cricket from the hill.

I took the cricket to the man in the village and told him I got a spirit from the holy place on the hill. The man opened the box, looked at me and then looked at the cricket. He said, "I have not seen such a beauty in a long time." He was very happy. The next day, the cricket man told me the medicine man wanted to see me. The medicine man asked me where I got the cricket. I said, "I don't lie." "You have to come with me to the back room," he said. He made me stand in the middle of the room. He burned incense on coconut husks, walked around me, and blew the smoke in my direction while talking or praying to himself. The next thing he asked me to do was take my shorts off, and this was the only thing I had on. He washed my body with flower water. He gave me a towel to dry myself with. I could hear him in the other room praying. When he came back in the room, we sat on chairs facing each other. He was praying again; he stood up and started massaging my head. Then, he gave me a coin on a string with the words two and a half cent under Dutch rule. He told me to keep the token on me at all times. I asked him if I still could lose my mind. He said, "No, you are saved."

The cricket man won the tournament, and there was a big celebration in the village. I was working out with Norman at his house when a man from the village came looking for me. He said the cricket man wanted to see me. The cricket man asked what kind of reward he could offer me for bringing him the champion. I said, "Food is scarce, and there are so many Eurasians living in the village who don't have enough to eat." He said, "I'll talk with the village elders and see what we can do." They did help, but it was not much because food was scarce for everybody.

The cricket man asked me if I would take his champion back to the sacred place. On my way to the hill I saw somebody in the distance following me. On the hill, I went in the bamboo forest and came out behind the man. The man was standing by one of the graves looking for me, when I asked him if he was looking for me. The man turned pale and did not know what to say. When he got over the shock, he asked me how he was able to see me going up the hill, but I was able to come up behind him. I told him this was a holy place. He was visibly shaking.

"I want you to tell me who told you to follow me," I said. He said, "I can't tell you." "You know what can happen to you, this is a sacred place," I added. I said, "Let's go back to the village, and we will find out."

Then the man said, "It's the medicine man who made me follow you." I went straight to the medicine man's house. I told the man to wait outside. The medicine man was sitting in the front room when I walked in. He looked at me and said, "How dare you come in my house without permission." "I have to talk to you, why would you have somebody follow me to the sacred place?" I asked. "I did not," he said. I went outside and brought the man in. I said, "Somebody is lying." The medicine man changed his tune. The medicine man said to the man, "You were supposed to be the best tracker in the village." The man said, "This boy has special powers." I told the medicine man that I would not work with people that didn't trust me. I stayed away from the village for a while.

I went to Max and Sara, and they were happy to see me. Max invited me in the house. As usual, Sara brought snacks to the table. Max asked me where I had been all this time. I told him I had been doing business with the village people close to my house. Max said, "I heard about that, and now you are a holy man." I said, "Whatever, but I will not do business with them anymore." Then I told Max about the man who followed me, and the incident with the medicine man. Sara said a boy should not be wandering around at night in the fields by himself. "It's dangerous, and there are many evil spirits out there," she added. I looked at Max, Max was raised by a Dutch family, so he was not superstitious.

Sara went back to the kitchen and told me to come see her before I left. "Norman came by and told me a story about how you won respect in the village," Max said. I said, "What has that blabbermouth told you?" "He told me that you are teaching him Pentjak and that you are working out with him." I asked what was wrong with that. "That is not all Norman told me. I know the boy you fought is the strongest and best fighter in that village," he said. I told him that he was. "Excuse me," Max said with a smile, "You don't look like a fighter." "Because I'm skinny and sick with malaria?" I asked. I said, "I'm not a fighter, but I can stand my ground." "Is it true that your father taught you?" Max asked. I told Max that I do not lie, but I would not tell who my Master was. Max told me he knew all the masters on the island. I asked how many masters were in the villages. "None," Max said, "but most of the men know Pentjak." He told me that where I lived before there was only one Master in the area. I said, "How do you know where I lived before?" Max said, "I know a lot more than you think."

Max said, "Your master's name is Amat." I still didn't say anything. Then Max said, "Let me describe his house: it's a white house with green windows and a white picket fence near the paved road." I said, "I did not tell you, you found out." Max said, "I couldn't believe that he would teach somebody off the street, and then a Eurasian. You must be special." "I am, Sara loves me!" I joked. Max said, "I meet with the masters sometimes." "Would you tell my master that I'm well?" I asked.

Sara called me to the kitchen, and said it's getting dark and it's a long walk home. She gave me a basket full of goodies. I said, "You want me to bring this to the Japanese, they are hungry." Sara pinched me on the cheek and said, "You know better, now go." I dropped some of the goodies at the Eurasian house in the village. They never asked where or how I got them. Some of the ladies said with tears in their eyes, "Someday you will eat at my house." Somehow, I didn't have to work for the Japanese much anymore. It seemed that the village chief skipped my name a lot. I didn't know whether Max had something to do with it, but when I did have to work it was always with the horses, which was an easy job.

One day, when I was visiting with Max, he told me the cricket master was very sorry for what happened. He told me he knew him well, and he was a good and honest man. "He wants to make things right with you," he said. "Yeah," I said, "Now he is a champion, he doesn't want me to go to another master." "That could be, but he wants to make it up to you," Max continued. He said, "The people in the village miss you too." I told Max, "This way, I can spend more time with Sara and get fat." Max shook his head. "All I want is for the medicine man and the cricket man to apologize to me," I said. "But I will not promise that I will find champions for them again," I continued.

Norman and I were scouting for birds. There were three large, tall, bamboo barns where there were many kinds of birds. The barns were used for drying the tobacco leaves. The tobacco fields and barns were not well taken care of. The people running them didn't know as much as the Dutch. We could go inside and there were bird droppings in the barns. I did the pitch trick that I learned from Jim. Norman was able to supply the bird feed, so we caught birds every time. The little grain-eating birds got stuck on the sticks, but some of the wild pigeons would fly away after losing some feathers. I always gave the catch to Norman.

Norman asked, "Do you ever run out of tricks?" I said, "It all depends on what you have in mind." Norman said, "The rivers have no more fish, but I know a stream on private property that has lots of fish." I said, "Use a fishing pole and bait." Norman said, "I did, but I want lots of fish." "Use a throw net," I said. Norman said, "I don't know how." I told Norman to take me to the stream. Norman told me we would have to leave early because it was a long walk. We came to a small village in the middle of nowhere. Norman walked right through the closed gates while there were people working in the field. Norman waved at them and kept on walking. I asked Norman, "Don't you have to ask permission to go through their fields?" Norman said, "No, the property belongs to my folks." The stream was clean with many fish in a holding section. I asked Norman what all the fish were for. Norman said, "My father wants to have a harvest party." He explained that his father had enough meat and chicken but couldn't get enough fish. I asked why his father didn't just buy them at the market. "My father said there was not much fish at the market, and when he buys the fish at the market, there is not enough to go around," Norman explained. I told Norman I thought I could help, but I needed him to give me time. "You have three weeks," Norman said.

The next day, Norman came over and told me his father wanted to talk to me. This was the first time I came face to face with Norman's father. He told me to sit down, then told Norman to leave the room. He looked at me and said, "For a young man you have lots of knowledge about nature." I told him that I grew up in the dessa village and those people were my mentors. He asked me if I was using the roots of a certain plant. I said, "No, that kills the fish and ruins the stream," I said. "You know that the roots are against the law," he said. "Yes, under Dutch law," I said. "And the stuff you are using now is against the law too, isn't?" he asked. I did not answer. Then he said, "I need fifty kilos of fish," and he got up and left.

Norman was waiting for me outside wanting to know what his father had said. "He wants fifty kilos of fish," I said. "How are you going to get fifty kilos of fish out the river?" he asked. "Aren't you helping me?" I asked. "What can I do?" Norman replied. "You have to make a net or get the materials for it," I said. I drew a picture on the ground of what the net would look like. Norman said, "I can have that made. We have lots of servants." I said, "Now you have to go back to the river." I told him the part of the river we would attack first. "Are you not coming with me?" he asked. I told him to make sure that the net reached from riverbank to riverbank and had strong stakes and a strong rope. Norman said, "When things go wrong, you're going to blame me." "Do it right and nobody is to blame," I said.

I went looking for the beans I needed to poison the fish. I knew that the plants grew at the edge of the woods. I found many plants and the beans were ready for harvest. I picked what I needed, dried them in the sun, roasted and ground them. They looked and smelled almost like coffee grounds. I checked on Norman and the net. It looked workable. I said, "Now we need worms, lots of worms." Norman looked at me, and said, "I don't know what you are up to, but I'll go along with it." "I need a five-gallon bucket with worms, and we have to be at the river before daylight," I said. I told him we would need to leave very early. Norman said, "No, I can do better, we will leave in the afternoon and stay in the village for the night. Then I will ask some of the men to help us string the net." Norman had one of the servants dig up the worms. I told him to line the bucket with banana leaves first. We were ready to leave. Norman had one of his horses packed with our supplies and his mother made sure that we had enough to eat and drink. I had some bamboo baskets that water could seep through to scoop up the fish. The villagers welcomed us and made it as comfortable as possible. There was no electricity and no running water.

The next morning, I showed Norman the ground-up beans. Norman said, "It is not possible to catch fish with coffee grounds." "You will find out," I said. We chopped up the worms, and I mixed my potion in with the worms and put them back in the bucket wrapped in banana leaves. Norm showed his disappointment and the natives were skeptical too. The net was set, and I walked upstream and threw the worms by the handful in the water. Now, it was a waiting game. It seemed like a very long time. Norman and the natives made fun of me, and Norman told me his father would be very disappointed. I saw some ripples and told them to get their scoops ready. Then it broke loose. They could not get the fish and other aquatic critters into the holding pen fast enough.

After four hard hours it was over. The holding pen was full, the net was full, and we were all tired. A woman came to us at the river and said, "The rice is cooking and I'm ready to fry fish." I told Norman we needed to clean the dead ones and fry them. Then, I told him to keep the other fish in the pen in the river. After the fish fry, I said to Norman, "You'll take care of everything from here on, and I'll go home." Norman said, "I'm sorry that I thought you would fail at the river."

After the harvest feast, Norman came to my house and said his father wanted to talk to me. "First of all, I want to thank you for the fish," he said. "Did you get enough?" I asked. "I asked for fifty kilos, and Norman came back with a lot more," he said. "I have no control of that," I said. "I have the rest salted and dried, you can have some of it," he said. Then he asked me if the rest of the stream was poisoned. I told him it wasn't, and after the rainy season the stretch of river would be full of fish again.

As usual, Norman was telling people that I had taught him how to catch fish with coffee grounds and worms. I let him believe it. Only his father knew what I actually used. I went to Max and Sara and told them I wanted to hide for a few days. Max asked, "What did you do this time?" "I want to get away from Norman; he asks too many questions that I can't answer," I said. Max said, "Now you can catch fish with coffee grounds?" "Norman really spread the word, didn't he? Now, you understand why I want to hide," I said. Max said, "I would like to know too." I said, "It is not coffee grounds." Sara said, "You can stay here, and I won't tell anybody."

The medicine man, cricket master and I were friends again. The medicine man told me that I must have special powers because I had done so much for the villagers already. The villagers didn't know as much as Jim, so I was fortunate that he taught me so many things. It was cricket time again, and the villagers were in the fields at night looking for crickets. One day, I was on the hill where the holy graves were, and I was digging for mole crickets. The natives didn't like to go up there. I got a string full of mole crickets. It was so nice and quiet that I cut some banana leaves to lay on. Then, I heard fighting crickets chirping. I thought that I was dreaming, but then I heard it again, which was strange. I remembered Jim telling me about the male birds that would stake out their territory and tell other males to stay away. It had nothing to do with spirits. I caught both crickets, they were big black ones. At home, I put them in a box.

The next day, I went to the cricket master and asked him if he had any good fighting crickets. He said he did. I said, "Then, you don't need my crickets, I think I'll take them to town and find them a master." He said, "I don't want you to do that." I showed him the crickets. He told me that they were so big that it would be hard to find a match for them. I said, "But easy to find a master for them." I said, "When is the big tournament? Maybe, I can enter them myself and fight them against yours." I could see that the cricket master did not like it, but he did not say anything. Then, I said, "I caught them for you, I will never deal with another cricket master."

There was a young man who stayed with us sometimes, he called my mother mom and thought of me as his big brother. He said to me, "I heard from mom that you stay out all night to find crickets." I told him that was true. He said, "You need protection, the next time you go out, I'll go with you." I said, "I don't need protection, I've been out there many times. I go where the natives don't dare to go, I go to the hill where the holy graves are and catch the spirits of the holy men who are buried there." He said, "How do you know that they are the spirits?" I told him that was what the natives told me. He asked if I believed them, and I said that I did. I introduced my so-called brother to the cricket master. The cricket master said, "You have a helper." I said, "No, he is my brother and he thinks that I need protection when I'm out there." We had some tea and snacks.

One night, my brother and I came home from our cricket hunt and the back door of the house was locked.

We did not want to wake up anyone, so we slept on a table in the hallway. The next morning, my mother came looking for us. I asked her what the deal was with locking the door. She said, "Last night, I got kissed by a horse." I said, "That only could happen to you." Apparently, one of Norman's horses got loose and came to our back door.

The cricket master said, "There is a spirit at the big cemetery where only the people who could afford it are buried. Do you know where that is?" I said, "Yes, I know, but the gates are locked at night and the walls are too high to climb, and the walls have pieces of glass cemented in." The cricket master told me there was a small gate on the side that was not locked. He told me that before I went up there, he wanted to warn me about a ghost who had scared everybody away who had tried. It was a dark night when my brother and I went looking for the crickets. We stopped to listen when all of a sudden a howling sound started, and something big was standing right next to us. My protector was out of the cemetery in no time. I froze, I could not run, but I shined my flashlight in the direction of the sound. I saw a man standing on top of a grave in a sarong with his arms stretched out like a scarecrow. I also saw that the man was a leper; he had no upper lip or nose. He asked me for a cigarette, and I told him that I didn't smoke, but would bring him cigarettes tomorrow night. I asked him why he was sleeping at the cemetery. He said, "Here is the only place where people leave me alone, but now that you have found out, they will chase me away from here too." I said, "Your secret is safe with me, I won't tell anyone."

I came out of the cemetery and saw my brother sitting under a streetlight looking down and holding his head. I yelled at him, and he jumped up. I looked at his legs and asked how many tombstones he had knocked down.

He said, "I don't want to talk about it, but I'm happy to see you." I said, "Yeah, when I needed protection where were you?" He said, "I had to fight my way out. I've never been so scared in my life." The next day, I asked him if he wanted to go to the cricket master with me. He said, "No, I have had enough of it." I went to the cricket master and told him that I went to the cemetery but did not catch the spirit. I told him I would not be going back. He asked if the ghost had scared me away, and I said yes.

I went to Max and Sara and told them about the leper at the cemetery. "He doesn't want anybody to know that he is up there at night, and that is why I want to bring him some cigarettes and food," I told them. Sara said, "You have a good heart, come back tomorrow evening, and I'll have something ready." I went back to the same place in the cemetery, but he was not there. I turned my flashlight on, and then I heard somebody hitting something. I turned my light off and walked in the direction of the sound. I found him. He said, "I did not believe that you would come back." I said, "I have something for you." He said, "You are an angel sent from heaven; you don't know how hungry I am." I said, "I know, and I will be back more often." He told me when I came back to not shine the light as much and he would guide me to where he was. I asked why he was always moving. "Ghosts don't stay in one place, you know," he joked. I visited him many times, but one night he was not there, and I never saw him again.

I went back to work for the Japanese taking care of the horses, but things had changed. The Japanese were friendly and working side by side with us. I asked the other workers what was going on. They did not know, but the Japanese were working harder than us. It looked like the Japanese were gathering everything and were ready to move out. I went to Max and asked him what was going on. Max told me America had bombed the Japanese with a very strong bomb, the atomic bomb, and there were many casualties. The Japanese surrendered. "What will happen now?" I asked. Max said, "I think there will be a lot of trouble if the Dutch army doesn't come here soon. He explained that during the Japanese occupation the Japanese told the Indonesians that Asia belonged to the Asians, and that they had to get rid of the colonials and their descendants because they have robbed Asia for hundreds of years. The only good thing for me was that the Japanese soldiers had taught me the art of Judo.

THE INDONESIAN REVOLUTION (1945-1947)

THE JAPANESE RELEASED THE people out of the internment camps. These camps were scattered all over the island. People with relatives living outside the camps went back to living with their relatives. It was difficult for those without relatives to find housing. It was not uncommon to find four to five families or about twenty to twenty-five people living in a small house with a one-car garage.

Food was already scarce. While in camp they knew they would be fed, as little as that might be. Now they didn't know where their meals would be coming from and the relatives could not always feed them. Everybody was helping, including the natives. There was no Red Cross or any other organization.

I went to Max and Sara. I asked Max, "What will the future hold for us Eurasians?" Sara said, "Before you start a conversation with Max you come to the kitchen with me. You look hungry and pale." She made me a big meal. I said, "Malaria got ahold of me again. My servants made a concoction from young papaya leaves and made me drink it. It tasted awful." Sara said, "You know we have medicine." I said, "I was too sick, and nobody knows that you are my mother." Sara pinched me and with tears in her eyes she said, "I wish you would never leave." Max said, "Let me cut your hair." As always, Max kept my hair very short. A comb was a luxury for me.

Max said, "Things are not looking good for us Indos." He explained that the west and other big cities were occupied by British, Churkas, Australians, Dutch and some American troops. In the occupied places life was almost normal. The prisoners of war were well taken care of. The educated Indonesians and city people were forming an army. They were recruiting with propaganda and worked to recruit as many villagers as possible to make them fanatics. There was sporadic fighting, but the new Indonesian army, with their bamboo spears and machetes, were no match against the allied troops. Nobody knew when the allied troops would be here. In the meantime, things only got worse for the Eurasians in the unoccupied territories. Max game me some clothes that the natives wore: shorts, sarong, shirt and hat. Max told me to wear the clothes and take the back road through the village, not to go out my front door. I blended in well with the natives in the clothes Max gave me.

The new Indonesian army got bigger by the day. They patrolled the streets and villages chanting insults toward us Eurasians and forbade their native friends from doing business with us. Many Indos had Indonesian family who were able to help. The ones without Indonesian family would have starved without the help from their native friends. In the morning before daylight, our servants would check the fence for food wrapped in banana leaves left by the natives.

I only visited Max and Sara in the dark of night. One night, Max told me that the Indonesians declared war on us Eurasians. We had no weapons, and the only men left were old and just released from Japanese prison camp. There were some fights, but not in our neighborhood. There were some casualties among the Eurasians. The Japanese army put a stop to it. The Indonesian army was no match for the Japanese. They came to an agreement, no more killing, but the Indonesians put the Eurasians as prisoners of war in internment camps. Max said, "I advise you to stay home. You never know what could happen when they catch you." Sara was crying, she gave me a hug and said, "If I never see you again, I will never forget you."

Not long after my visit with Max and Sara, the trucks came and picked up all the men – my brother was one of them – and imprisoned them somewhere. My mother must have had a feeling because she started packing things and giving things away to our servants and native friends. I got malaria again, and I was not well for days. At night, the family and servants sat together in the dark burning mosquito repellent hoping to see daylight the next morning.

Then one night, there was so much noise that it sounded like a war. We were all huddled together hoping that the Japanese wouldn't shoot at us. Then Norman came over and told us that the tobacco barns were on fire, all three of them, and invited me to come and watch. There were so many people from the kampongs watching, but the Japanese soldiers kept them at a distance. The noise of the bamboo exploding was very impressive to me. There was no way to fight the fire. The flames and cinders flying high up into the sky against the bright orange glow was a sight I will never forget. It took many days to burn out.

The servants told my mother if we got picked up, they would come with us. The trucks came to pick us up, and we were ready. My mother had things packed and told the servants they could have what was left. The young soldiers with the bamboo spears were very rude. Then they told my mother that I had to go to another camp; only children under twelve could stay with their mothers. My mother and the servants told the soldiers that I was too sick and could not take care of myself. They gave my mother time to pack some stuff for me. The servants were not allowed to go with my mother.

The men were put in a military camp that used to be a car dealership. The bunks were two and three high with a tin roof, no ventilation, and the daytime temperature was around one hundred degrees Fahrenheit. There was one faucet with one light above it, and that was the only light in the whole complex. The faucet was set on a small stream. It could not be adjusted, and it ran day and night. It was the only water to be had for all the people. There was not enough water to take a bath, and with the heat this was trouble. Day or night there were always men standing in line for water.

The outhouses were built above a dry creek, far behind the buildings in an open field. They were small bamboo huts with a hole in the floor, which was difficult for the older men. The fence by the outhouses had holes in it, so you could hear and see the traffic and people on the outside. Sometimes, we traded things for food with the people on the outside. To get to the outhouse you had to pass the guardhouse, but you didn't have to bow for the guard like you did with the Japanese. The guardhouse had running water and floodlights that reached all the way to the fence by the outhouses. They would use the floodlights only when they suspected us of trading. The guards would not beat us; they would just take the food away. The guards never went back to the outhouses because of the smell. We were very generous when trading with outside people.

Everybody expected to be rescued by the allied troops in a very short time. Every day at 6:00 a.m. we had to stand in line for a head count. Even if we could escape there was no place to hide. Once a day, there were six to eight men pulling an ox cart going to the women's camp. The women were placed in a convent and cooked for the men's camp. To and from the camps the men had to endure a lot of brutality from the people who hated us. If it wasn't for the guards who had firearms, they might attack them.

The first day in camp my next-door neighbor from when I was a child found me. We had gone to school together. Since I was sick, he took care of me, he would get the food, which was never enough, and stood in line for water. When I was well enough to be up and around, I was always hungry, but there was nothing to eat.

After a month or so, it started to sink in that we might be in camp for a long time. One night, we were rounded up and put in trucks and transported to another camp. We drove all night and part of the next day, but we could not see outside. We arrived at the prison camp. It was a plantation, and we lived in the housing complex for the staff employees. Under Dutch rule, it must have been a beautiful place. It had not been taken care of in recent years. It must been empty for some time as there was tall grass in the lawns, overgrown garden plots, weeds and brush as tall as the fence with barbed wire on top by the guardhouse gate. The houses were empty. There was no electricity, no running water, and cement floors. There were two deep wells with clean water, and a river running through the property. The outhouses were little bamboo huts in the field away from the buildings.

There were some Dutch men who had been in Japanese prison camp. We also had men from other prison camps. I lost my friend; he and the other men were transported to other camps. The men were forming groups and staking out places. I was with a good group. I was the youngest of the group, and the men kept things organized. We could get along with the guards. The guards were all educated Indonesians who spoke Dutch, and some of them felt sorry for us. There was a big kitchen in the camp where they used wood for fuel. The men who prepared the food had to do it in fifty-gallon drums. The food was the same every day, steamed rice and boiled greens. There was no salt or seasoning in the food. Sometimes, there were bugs or grubs floating in the boiled greens. The first in line would get them; it was the only meat we got. The food was never enough, everybody was always hungry.

After two months, the overgrown fields with the bugs, snakes, mice, rats, squirrels and birds were a thing of the past. Every day some of us would sit in the grass, pull the green part off and eat the white part. Everybody urinated at a designated place, and nothing would grow there. The group of men who had to supply the kitchen their fuel had to go outside camp and cut wood in the overgrown plantation with axes, machetes and ropes. There were no chainsaws.

Every morning after headcount, the woodcutters would go with the guards to go out and find wood. I was one of the lucky ones who got to go with them. My job was picking up the wood chips and putting them in a basket to carry back to the kitchen. In the woods there were always wild fruit, berries, and edible plants to be found. The guards were not very strict. They let me roam around in the woods. Every branch of a tree was being used. After the woodcutters cut and split the wood, we volunteers would come and carry the wood to the kitchen.

One day we were cutting wood close to a stream, and as usual I was scouting around. I went down the ravine to the river to see if I could find anything. The riverbank was overgrown, and to my surprise I found a python asleep in a big hole in the rock wall. Back in camp, I told the woodcutters about the snake in the rock wall at the river. The woodcutters asked me how big it was. I said I didn't know but the head looked bigger than mine. "That's a lot of meat," they said. They asked me if I knew a way to kill that monster. I said, "No, I'm afraid." Jim never taught me how to catch a snake that big. The woodcutters made a snare from a small cable and a long water pipe. There were grooves cut in the pipe where I could fasten the cable, so it wouldn't slip, and a long rope that I had to fasten to a tree.

The next day in the woods, the men told me to go down to the river and snare the monster. Normally, I'm not afraid, but this time I was very afraid. When Jim told me to do things, I knew it would work. However, I knew my men were counting on me. When I got to the snake it was still lying in the same position as when I saw it days before, but now I could see its tongue was coming out of its mouth. I knew the snake was awake and could tell that something was close by. First, I fastened the long rope to a tree. I had no problem putting the snare behind the snake's head. Then I pulled the cable as tight as I could and fastened the cable to the pipe. I jumped in the river and watched from a distance, but nothing happened. The snake pulled itself deeper in the hole. I did not wait.

The woodcutters asked me how it went. I told them I put the snare behind the snake's head, but nothing happened, and then we had to leave. The next day, the woodcutters sent me down to the river to check on the snake. I was very surprised to see what happened at the river. The brush at the riverbank was flattened and the snake, which was bigger than anything I had seen before, was in the river, not dead. I told the woodcutters that the snake was in the river, but it wasn't dead. I told them that I was not going back there alone. Two strong woodcutters went down to the river with a big basket. When I saw the basket again, the snake was already covered with wood chips. I never saw the snake up close. Late that night, somebody came over to my group and brought a big chunk of roasted snake meat.

Sometimes, we cut wood close to a small village. One day, I was looking for dry wood and wandered off from the woodcutters. I heard a voice and I looked up and saw an old woman standing behind a bush. She pointed to a house close to the woods and told me to go to there and she would meet me. In the house, she told me where to sit, so she could see if somebody was coming. I asked her why she was doing this. She told me that she used to take care of the white children living in the big house that was now the prison camp. She explained that under Dutch rule they were poor, but the Indonesians all had work. Then she added that the Japanese did not take care of the plantation, and now the Indonesians had no work and hardly any food. She gave me a bowl with warm steamed rice and a piece of dried salted fish. I told her I couldn't eat her food because I didn't want her to go hungry. She told me she wanted me to eat it. I obliged, and it tasted so good. Then I told her that we could not get salt in the camp. She gave me a brick of salt and told me it was all she had. Again, I told her I couldn't, but she wrapped it in a banana leaf and told me to go. I hid the salt in the dry wood I had gathered. I never told the woodcutters about the salt. Salt was very valuable in camp, and now my food would taste better.

Many men had Indonesian relatives living outside the camps. Our guards gave them permission to visit their relatives in camp once a month in the guardhouse. One day, I was called to the guardhouse, and they told me that my uncle came to visit. I had no relatives outside, and to my surprise it was Max. However, if anybody would do it, it would be him. Knowing Sara, she packed a lot of dried fish, meat, vegetables and rice. She also put a pan and to cook with, a water canteen, and malaria medicine. Max did not ask how I was doing. He asked if I needed other things. I told him salt, and a blanket or sarong would be very helpful because it was very cold at night. Max asked me what happened to the stuff my mother packed. I told him it was all gone. I explained that I traded all my stuff for food because I was not expecting to be held prisoner for such a long time. I asked how Sara was doing. He said she was sad and every time my name came up, she cried. I told him to tell her I thought of her every day. Max told me the village people still talked about me and told him to give me their best wishes. I asked how Norman and David were doing. Max told me David was in hiding and Norman had joined the Indonesian army.

The visits lasted until we got a new group of guards. The new guards were bad. No more visitors from outside. After morning roll call, the woodcutters had to walk single file without talking. They were imitating the Japanese. In the woods, the guards were always close by. No more wandering around and looking for things to eat for me. They were not carrying firearms, but they were always looking for an excuse to use their bamboo spears or sticks on us. The insults went on and on every day. The woodcutters got very tired of it.

One day, there was talk about overpowering the guards to teach them a lesson. There were fifteen of us including me, and only five of them with bamboo spears and sticks. The woodcutters were working close together, and the guards started their daily insults. The woodcutters talked back like never before. The other guards came to see what was going on. That was when they got overpowered, their sticks taken away, and their hands tied behind their backs. The woodcutters made them sit back to back and tied all their hands together, so they could not stand up. The leader of the woodcutters picked up a spear and walked up to the leader of the guards. He put the point of the spear to his throat and said, "this is the way we kill pigs." For an Indonesian to be called a pig was a tremendous insult. The woodcutters picked up their things and went back to camp.

The guards started yelling and begging the woodcutters not to leave them in the woods. The woodcutters went straight to the guardhouse and asked to speak to the commander. The commander asked what they wanted. The woodcutters told him that they had troubles with the guards. The woodcutters told him that they had overpowered the guards and left them tied up in the woods. The commander asked which one was the leader. Two of them stepped forward. The commander told them to come to his office with the spears.

In his office, the commander spoke Dutch to the woodcutters. He told them they should be severely punished, but he wanted to know what really happened. The woodcutters told the commander that the young soldiers made it impossible to work with them. They told the commander that as soon as they left the gate each day the soldiers would start insulting them in Dutch. Then they told him that in the woods they would always look for any excuse to stroke us with their canes. They mentioned a time when a man was taking down a tree, and a guard told him that the cut was wrong, so he started stroking him with the cane while the man still had an ax in his hands. Then the guard went to the stacks of wood, pushed them over because they were not stacked right, then started hitting the stackers. After that the guards took it out on the boy who picked up the wood chips. They kicked his basket over, then worked on him. The told the commander things like this happened every day, until they just could not take it anymore.

The commander said he would take care of the matter himself. He told the two leaders to come with him, and he ordered another guard to go with them all. In the woods, the commander was very angry and let the soldiers know. He told the woodcutters to cut them loose. They walked back to the guardhouse without a word being said. At the guardhouse the commander asked the woodcutters to come to his office again. He spoke to them in Dutch and wanted to know how they could work together. The woodcutters said that they could get more work done without guards. The commander told them to come back to his office after roll in the morning. The next morning, only one guard carrying a rifle came with us. Work got done.

One morning, the commander was at roll call and told us to be ready to move at nightfall. The trucks came and the old, the sick and the weak were loaded in trucks with only some of the young and healthy. We were waiting for transportation, but we were wrong. The guards carrying firearms told us we had to walk. We walked all night without food or water. I stayed with my group and the woodcutters. By daylight, we came by a small village, and it seemed that everybody from the village was standing on the side of the road. These people, under Dutch rule, had worked at the plantations for generations, and they still liked the Dutch.

The guards were as tired and hungry as we were. The guards asked the village people for drinking water. We rested a bit and drank water. The women gave us fruit to take with us. The guards did not stop them. It was getting very hot, but we kept walking. We came to a place where many side roads came together. The guards said we should rest there because it was a nice, cool and shady place. We lay down and slept. We continued our journey. Along the way we heard and saw many birds and some wildlife. Under Dutch rule, when the plantations were taken care of, it must have been very beautiful. In the distance, we saw dust clouds and knew the trucks were on their way. It was a long ride to our new prison camp.

When we arrived at the new prison camp it was almost dark. We had to find a place to sleep for the night. We had not eaten for almost two days. The next morning at roll call, I saw many new faces, many older men who had been released from Japanese prison camp. This camp was big, and there were many houses, big and small, and a big empty warehouse. There were roads in this camp that the officers used. They drove a jeep through camp to make the rounds. There were many open fields with lots of edible greens, a creek going through the property and three deep wells with clean water for drinking and cooking. The kitchen was close to the creek, and they used wood for cooking. There were two guardhouses, one at the front entrance and one at the back entrance. Behind the fence were more houses that were used as a military camp. The prison camp has its own leaders, and every group has its own leader. The woodcutters and my group stayed together in a small house close to the kitchen and the river. Finally, food was served, the same thing as always, rice and boiled greens. I was so hungry, and it was gone before I knew it.

This camp was in the mountains, and the nights could be cold. Lucky for me, Max had brought me a blanket and a sarong when I was in the previous camp. The woodcutters got their jobs back. There were two crews because the woodcutters had to supply fuel for the prison and the military camp. A woodcutter was assigned to our group. He was a little older than the men in our group. He knew what he was doing in the woods and was a hard worker.

I got a malaria attack, and the sarong and blanket could not keep me warm. Our leader threw more blankets on me. After roll call, he came back to check on me. I told him that I had quinine powder, and he got me water. He told me that he was a doctor. This group of men took good care of me. They made sure that I had something to eat every day. I told our leader that I had a brick of salt. I said I wanted to share it with everybody in our group. I gave him the salt. He told me it was worth more than gold. "Yes, I would rather have salt!" I said.

In this camp, I met a man who was severely tortured in Japanese prison camp. It seemed to me that the Japanese broke every joint in his hands, arms, feet, and legs. They had pulled all his nails out. He could hardly walk or carry anything, and he had a hard time talking because he had a hole in his throat.

I went back to the woods with the woodcutters. The guards carried firearms. In the woods, they let us do whatever we wanted as long as we supplied enough wood. In comparison with the regular prisoners our life was good. Just before dark, there were many bats flying low through camp. These were not the giant fruit bats, so there were many men with long sticks with branches attached to the top waiting for them. It reminded me of the time that I was running after kites, but now it was serious business. When they caught a bat, they would throw it on the fire and consume it. Some of these bats were so small, not any bigger than my thumb.

I liked the stories the older woodcutter told me. He told me that he lived on government land. He did not pay rent or taxes, and it was a big piece of land. He built a house and dug a deep well. He collected rainwater in big wooden containers. He worked the land and cut timber out of the forest. He had some chickens, goats, sheep and a couple of oxen for the heavy work. He had no family and very seldom went to town. I asked him what kind of wildlife he had where he lived and if he ever trapped some of them. He told me the wildlife by his place were wild boar, deer, wild chickens, doves and pigeons. "That is my meat supply," he said. I asked if he shot them. "No," he said, "When you shoot them, they will not come back for a long time, so I trap them." "How do you do that?" I asked. "Why are you so interested?" he asked. I said, "I have trapped birds, but never big game." I told him how I used to trap birds.

He told me he did it differently where he lived. Wild boar was the main meat supply. He told me he caught the wild boar two different ways. "First, I dig a pit in the ground where they feed, and this is a permanent pit. When I need meat, I take the cover off and replace it with a light cover and put some food on the cover. When I check the trap, I always have a pig or two in the pit. I take the one I want and free the other ones. I marinate the meat and dry it in the sun," he explained. "My second trap is a net fastened to a loaded pole or tree. Most trappers use a snare for this. I use a net because it will not harm the animal. While eating, the boar will trigger the net, and the next thing you have a pig hanging in the air unharmed with legs sticking out of the net. I keep the area supplied with food," he added. I remembered wild boar meat tasted good. When I was a little boy, my father used to shoot them, and our servants did the same thing with the meat.

Then he told me he didn't use pitch to catch birds. He had baskets with holes small enough so that the birds wouldn't slip through, and a door on top. He told me he put them in front of his window. Then he propped one side of the basket up with a stick and had a string going into the house that was tied to the stick. There was always feed in and around the traps. The wild chickens and birds would feed there every day. He told me if he wanted a chicken or bird all he had to do was pull the string. Then he told me that sometimes he would guide hunters. He always took them far away from his place. They never stayed long after they shot their pig, and he would butcher and pack the meat and they would be on their way. I asked him if he ever got lonely. He told me sometimes in the rainy season, but he would make furniture and paint. "What do you paint?" I asked. "Landscapes," he said; "there is a lot of beauty in nature."

With the other woodcutters there was a young man about my age. We called him the bee man. Whenever we found a beehive, he would get the honey. He was not allergic to bee venom. All he had for protection was mosquito netting over a tropical helmet fastened around his neck, and smoke to prevent the bees from stinging him in the face. When he was taking the honeycombs out of the beehive the bees would be swarming so thick that we could hardly see him. After he finished taking the honeycombs out of the beehive, we helped him take the stingers out. Wherever he got stung we put vinegar on the sting. We ate the honeycombs with the larvae, and the rest went to the kitchen where they would extract the honey. The honey stayed with the woodcutters and the kitchen workers. Some of the honey we would trade for vinegar with the guards.

If a beehive was high up in the tree the woodcutters would take the tree down first. However, the pounding of the ax against the tree made the bees mad and they would come swarming out before the tree was down. The woodcutters found other places to cut wood. The older woodcutter asked the guard if he could go in the woods early in the morning to cut the bee trees down before the bees were active. After he cut the bee trees down, he would go to the place we worked the day before. Our bee man said to wait a day and let the bees settle down. When he found the queen, he would put her somewhere, where she was comfortable, and most of the bees would follow her. It made his job so much easier.

When there was enough wood or when it rained too much we wouldn't go in the woods. The woodcutters worked on their tools, and I helped in the kitchen when needed. When I didn't go in the woods and the kitchen didn't need me, I would wander around in camp and make new friends. I met a boy I went to school with; as a matter of fact, we had sat on the same bench in fourth grade. His name was Victor. Victor said that he was in prison camp with his father. His father was old and sick. Victor was afraid that without medicine his father would die. Victor had asked the guards if they could get him medicine for his father. The guards told him that they could not supply medicine or a doctor for the prison. I talked with the doctor in my group about Victor's father. The doctor told me he was already working on a project for the old and sick, but without medicine there wasn't much he could do.

The doctor had asked the people that caught rats and other rodents if he could boil them and take the stock to give to the sick and the weak. The people were convinced that the doctor was helping the sick. They brought the rodents already cleaned. The doctor said that I could help him when I was not busy. The doctor boiled the rodents in my pan without asking. He gave the meat back, then he brought the stock to a boil again, with a little of my salt, celery and onion that he got out of the guards' kitchen. He strained it through mosquito netting and gave it to the sick.

I found some dried-up celery plants in the old garden plot close to the kitchen. I told the kitchen crew about it. They said they would bring the plants back to life and take care of them. I went back in the woods, and this time of the year there were many ripe fruits. Every day during this season I would pick fruit and take it to camp. The guards did not stop me. I found coffee plants with ripe beans. The ripe coffee beans tasted sweet. The coffee people drank was the ground-up roasted seed.

One day the woodcutters were not going in the woods,

so I was roaming around in camp. I saw Victor turning the ground with a patjul, an agricultural tool. He did not want to talk to me and told me to get lost. I went to the doctor and helped him. I asked the doctor what was going on with Victor. The doctor said Victor's father died and was buried there. Victor did something that required punishment, I don't know what it was. His punishment was to turn the entire field; it was one hectare, approximately 100 meters by 100 meters. It was a big field and the ground was hard. It had not been worked for a long time. The doctor told me he only had three days to do it. I said he would never make it. Victor worked from early in the morning until dark. He only took a break when the meal was served. He got the job done in time. After his father's death Victor changed; he was always by himself. He didn't mingle with other people. When Victor and I were in school, he was always athletic. We were altar boys, boy scouts, and we played soccer together. Now, it seemed like he didn't enjoy my friendship.

One morning, I woke up and could not open my eyes. I went to the creek and washed my eyes. The woodcutters told me that my eyes were very red. They told me to go to the doctor. The doctor told me I had a very contagious eye disease, and he had no medicine for it. I asked the doctor if I should stay away from everybody because I didn't want to contaminate others. He told me it did not matter because the disease was already here, and many people in camp already had it. I asked what would happen if I didn't find medicine for it. The doctor said at worst I would go blind, but most likely it would cure itself. The bright sunlight hurt my eyes, but in the woods, there was a lot of shade, which helped.

One of the guards noticed my eyes and told me I could

find medicine for it in the woods. He showed me the plant and told me that two weeks ago he had the same eye problems, and the leaves cured it. The guard told me to pick the healthy leaves, wash them, wilt them with heat, crush them, and squeeze the juice in my eyes. I showed the doctor the leaves and told him what the guard had told me. The doctor said, "I don't know anything about the leaves, but it's up to you." I went to the kitchen crew and asked them for help. We did it the way the guard told me. The first time, I did not feel anything, but the next morning my eyes were glued shut. I did it twice a day, and in five days my eyes were healed.

Life in prison camp was going downhill. There were many sick people, especially the older people who had been in Japanese prison camp for more than three years. Malaria was knocking on my door too. There was a dysentery epidemic in camp, and almost everybody was infected. I had it too. With dysentery, you had the urge to go, you would get painful cramps, you would wait and wait, but nothing came out but a little slime and a few drops of blood. This went on day and night; it was very hard on the body. It was everywhere; the kitchen crew, the woodcutters, everybody got it. Many older men could not make it to the outhouse, so they did it wherever it hit them. The flies were always on it. The doctor asked the able bodies to cover it up with dirt or ashes. There were so many sick people in camp that the doctors were worried, but helpless. They saw to it that everything was clean. The same guard who helped me with my eye problem told me to eat the young leaves from the guava tree and it would lessen the cramps. It helped when I had food in my stomach. It took a while before the men got well, and life in camp was routine again.

One day, we heard airplanes flying low and the guards made us stay out of sight. When we saw that the planes had Dutch and English flags on them, we ran to the open fields and waved with everything we could find. We knew that they saw us because we could see the pilots. The planes came back and dropped boxes, lots of boxes, that all fell in the prison camp. Every group was gathering the boxes for themselves. The guards did not stop us. The kitchen crew, woodcutters, and my group had a room full of boxes stashed away in our house. Every box had the same supplies in it. Everything was in cans or wrapped in paper. There was a big can with dehydrated corned beef, which was my favorite. The boxes had cheese, butter, coffee, chocolate, sugar, salt, pepper, cigarettes and a lot more.

Something was wrong: many people got sick, including me, and it was coming out of both ends. The doctors called a meeting with all the camp leaders. The doctors told them if they didn't take the food away people could die. They decided they needed to feed the good stuff to us slowly, so our systems could handle it. From my rations, I only kept the corned beef, uncooked rice, beans and salt. I traded the other parts of my ration for corned beef. For as long as it lasted, I had two meals a day. All good things come to an end, and the planes never came back. It was moving time again.

One evening, we were rounded up with what little belongings we had and loaded in trucks. We drove all night, and in the morning we came to a railroad station. At the station were military and civilians who had food ready for us. It was the first time that we got more than a few bites of rice. The fed us real vegetables, gave us water to drink and let us go to the bathroom. Then, it was into the train; they were third-class wagons with long wooden benches, one in the middle and two on the sides. The windows were nailed shut and the doors were closed – it was an oven. After just a few hours, there was a bad smell in the wagons. The next morning, the train stopped at a railroad station where we had to get off. Many of the old men needed help to get off the train.

We went through the same routine of food, water, potty break, but this time we also got to stand for a very short time under the faucet that supplied the steam locomotives with water. It was another long drive before we got to the prison camp. This prison camp was very big; it looked like a town if it wasn't for the fence and barbed wire. A section was set aside for us newcomers. We were so tired that we went in the houses and went right to sleep. It didn't take long before the mosquitoes and bedbugs were crawling all over us. We were not in the mountains anymore, and the nights were hot.

The next morning, we staked out our places in the buildings. We stayed together: kitchen crew, woodcutters, and us. We didn't get any food until 2:00 p.m. The food was still the same steamed rice and boiled greens, but in this camp, we got a little more. There was plenty of clean water, but not close to us. Water faucets were few and far between; instead there were many deep wells, but some were contaminated.

The story at the camp was that when the Indonesian army took over, the residents fought them. Depending on who you talked to, the residents were either Japanese or white. The dead were thrown in the wells. Then the wells were filled up with rocks, cement blocks, junk out of the houses like bathtubs, commodes, kitchen stuff and furniture. The houses had no electricity or running water. The kitchen crew did not get their jobs back. There was already a kitchen crew for this section. Every section had their own kitchen and the leaders managed their own area. Our section was section C. Morning roll call was done at our own section.

It seemed like all the prisoners from other camps were brought to this camp. I began to see many familiar faces from other camps I had been in before. My brother, whom I had not seen for a long time, was in this camp too. I stayed with my group because he was in another section of the camp. There were many openings in the fence that separated the prison from the village, but the men from prison and the village people always made the fence look solid. You could get a lot of stuff from outside if you had things to trade. Once you got the stuff into the camp the guards would not take it away unless they caught you red handed. Men with Indonesian relatives living outside of the prison were better off. The guards carrying firearms were supposed to patrol the fence 24/7.

One dark night, I traded my sarong for some duck eggs. It was so dark that I could not see very far in front of me. As I was hurrying away from the fence, I came around the corner of a building and bumped right into a guard. I dropped my basket with eggs and rolled in the tall grass. The guard had a flashlight, but he did not see me, the ground was sloped enough that I stayed hidden in the tall grass. Behind me was a big drop off into the dry creek where the outhouses were; it would have been a disaster if I had fallen in.

I told the doctor what happened, and he scolded me. He said, "You traded almost everything you have, your cooking pan is gone, your clothes are gone, the only thing you have is the shorts you have on, and who knows how long we will still be locked up. Someday you will be naked." I said, "There is so much you can get at the fence, and I'm hungry. I have two half coconuts for my food, and a hollowed-out piece of bamboo for my drinking water." The doctor said, "I don't want you to trade your blanket." I told him I was using my blanket for a pillow. The temptation was too strong, so I traded my blanket anyway.

Now I was totally broke, had nothing of value to trade, and I was still hungry. Without my blanket at night, I had no protection from the bed bugs and mosquitoes. When it got too bad, I would I walk aimlessly around at night. I got a malaria attack and did not get much sympathy from the doctor. I had no medicine, so when I was cold, I would lie in the sun, and when I was hot with fever, I would lie on the cement floor. When I was cold at night, I would ask the big guys to lie close to me, so that I could get some of their body heat. The worst were the headaches after a malaria attack. When I was too sick to stand in line to get my food somebody always got food and water for me.

The woodcutters didn't go in the woods because the logs were delivered. The logs were cut into sections, split and stored in a barn next to the kitchen. I collected the wood chips because they were used to start the fire. Sometimes, the woodcutters took trees down on the property. It was impossible to take a tree down in sections with an ax. When we had to take a tree down close to a building, we used ropes to guide the tree away from the building. The older woodcutter in our group was very good at this. I was a good climber, so he told me where to fasten the ropes and told the other woodcutters how to make the cuts. When the tree was ready to come down the other woodcutters kept tension on the ropes, and he was always the one who gave the tree the last chop with the ax. We never had a tree fall on a building.

The greens were delivered daily and dumped in front of the kitchen. I helped the kitchen crew sort out what was edible. The waste was collected by a man who had a still in the john. I don't know how he made the booze. There was a group of rednecks who liked to play music in the evening and drink alcohol. I tasted the booze; I did not like it. When the truck with the rice supply came, the kitchen crew and volunteers unloaded the trucks. One rice sack weighed 100 kilograms. The Indonesians who delivered the rice always made fun of the men who struggled unloading the heavy rice sacks.

One day, after days of heavy rains, a guard came to our group and asked for volunteers. He told us there was a mudslide at the river. Ten of us volunteered. We had never been outside the prison. Across the street was a big village; to get to the river we had to go through the village. At the river, we worked side by side with the villagers. The villagers were very friendly. The expertise of the older woodcutter made the work easier and faster. At break the women brought us lunch, plenty of rice with salted fish, coffee and tea with sugar. I can't describe how great it felt to eat real food and have a full belly. We worked from daylight to dark. The job only lasted two days, but it felt so good.

When it rained a lot, I went out looking for crickets, grubs, snails and other insects. Since I had no pan, I put the insects on a stick and roasted them. We also had many non-fruit trees on the property. Sometimes the big fruit bats ate fruit in those trees and dropped the half-eaten fruit. Every morning I looked for the fruit, but I was not the only one. One hot afternoon, I went to the guard and asked if they would let us swim in the river. To my surprise, he said only those who had worked at the river. The first day six of us went. I had hoped that the women would bring us food. They tried but the guard did not allow it.

Every day in the afternoon, some of us hung around the guardhouse hoping they would let us go to the river. It didn't always work. When we were in the river, we tried to catch fish or other critters without much luck. However, when we did catch something the guard let us keep it. One hot afternoon, I was alone hanging around the guardhouse hoping they would let us go to the river. I walked behind the guardhouse and saw some overripe bananas on top of the garbage pile. I picked them up and a side door opened. A voice said, "You don't pick things out of the garbage!" I threw the bananas back and saw an officer standing in the doorway. He gave me some of the bananas. I went back to my group and said, "Look what I got!" We ate the bananas on the spot. The man who had the still asked if he could have the banana peel, it gave his booze flavor, he said. Then he told us whenever we found any rotten fruit or peelings, he wanted it. I had a feeling that the officer was keeping an eye on me.

One day coming back from the river, a guard told me the commander wanted to see me. In his office, he said, "Do I know you?" I said, "If you tell me who you are, we might find out." He said, "A long time ago, when I was living with my pentjak Master, there was this white boy our Master let work out with us, and you look a lot like him." I looked up, but I did not recognize the man. I said, "Yes, I was given permission by my Master to be taught the martial art by two young men. We grew very close; we were like brothers." The commander told me he was one of them. "My heart bleeds to find you like this," he added. I asked him how our Master and the other young men were doing. He said, "Our Master is not making tempeh anymore, he is with the government and his other student is a schoolteacher."

I was picking up wood chips when a guard carrying a firearm told me the commander wanted to see me. My friends asked me what I had done. At the office the commander told me to sit down because there was somebody that wanted to meet me. I had a feeling who it was, so when he entered the room and sat down in front of me, I did not look up. He said, "I can't put into words how I feel to see you like this." I never looked up, I was crying and said, "I'm ashamed that you are seeing me like this, with long hair and really dark skin, living like an animal."

I asked my Master if he had seen Max and Sara. He said, "Yes, Max works for the government. Not long ago, we had a meeting at his house, and every time your name came up Sara would cry." I said, "Would you give them my best wishes? I think of them every day." The conversation made me think of the good old days, and I was sad when I left the office. My friends wanted to know what happened at the office. I said, "Nothing happened; they told me not to pick up stuff from around the guardhouse." I did not go swimming anymore, and my friends could not understand why. I did not want to come close to the guardhouse knowing that part of me was guarding the prison.

Time went by, then one day I was asked to come to the guardhouse. The first thing the commander, my brother, did was give me a hug, even though I was so dirty. Then he said I have something for you from the Master. He gave me a brown jar. I asked what was in it. He told me they were sugar-covered quinine pills, easy to swallow. I had never seen them before. He told me he wanted me to have a haircut. I said please do. There were sores from lice bites on my head and he put ointment on them. Then he told me that he would be replaced by another officer the next day. He said, "I hope when we meet again it will be in better circumstances." It never happened.

I showed the doctor my pills, and he asked how I got them. I told him somebody gave them to me. The doctor asked if he also cut my hair, and I said yes. The doctor said, "I don't believe this, but I won't question you." The doctor kept the pills, and I asked him why he was keeping the pills. The doctor said, "I don't trust you with them and I will see to it that you take two pills a day whether you are sick or not until all the pills are gone."

The new commander would not give us permission to swim in the river. I befriended some of the guards. Sometimes they let me and some men in my group help them stack wood and clean their kitchen. There was always fresh good food in their kitchen. I could not fight the temptation any longer, and I ate some of the food. Of course, I got caught. I got punished. I had to stack firewood and could not go to the guardhouse anymore. The guard I befriended told me if he had been in my place, he would have done the same thing.

I developed a rash right by my waistband, and it itched all the time. I asked the doctor what it could be. The doctor told me I had clothes lice. I asked what I could do to get rid of them. The doctor told me to ask the people with kerosene lamps if they could spare some kerosene. "Then what?" I asked. "Pour it on your pants and burn it," he replied. I looked at him but did not say anything. The doctor said, "Pour it on your waistband it might kill the lice." Nobody would give me kerosene. At night, I sat out of sight and soaked my pants in water. It did not help much. When my clothes dried the lice started biting again. The warmer it got the more active they got. When it got too bad, I sat in the shade and loosened my waistband, so the lice could not get to my skin.

One night, there was a lot of excitement in camp; they were taking roll call at night. We learned that there were men who escaped from our camp and tried to get into the women's camp. The women's camp was not far from our camp. The men got caught and punished. The fence had to be made escape-proof. We had to work on the fence, and again, our woodcutter was the expert in making the fence escape-proof. My feet and legs were a little swollen. I asked the doctor what it could be. He told me it was the beginning of beriberi. "What is that?" I asked. He told me it was from eating the same food and not getting enough vitamins, but not to worry.

MOVING INTO THE WOMEN'S CAMP

WE WERE INFORMED THAT all the men would be moved to the women's camp to be reunited with their families. When we arrived in the women's camp we were kept in a separate area until they figured out who belonged where. The men who did not have any family were kept separate. All the men I lived with for so long went their separate ways. The men I missed the most were the doctor and the woodcutter.

When I finally got reunited with my mother, she looked at me with tears in her eyes and said, "When you left, you were so sick that I thought that would I never see you again." I told her about all the men who took care of me when I needed help. I said, "I'm not in great shape but I'm alive." "Where are your belongings?" she asked. I showed her my two half coconuts and my bamboo canteen. "Where are your clothes?" she asked. I told her I traded it all for food. I told her about the clothes. I told her about the lice in my pants and showed her where they were biting me. She made me new clothes. They looked like a sack, with an opening for the head, arms, and legs with buttons in front. The fabric design was for women, it was black with red roses. I burned my pants. My mother made me one more with birds on it. I could change clothes and they were washed regularly.

I got a malaria attack, and I did not tell anybody, but you can't hide a malaria attack. When I had the chills, my mother would put lots of blankets on me. With the fever she would put wet towels on my forehead and sit by my side. It sure made a difference lying in the sun or on a cement floor. Life in this new internment camp was not bad.

All the people had to fill in papers. We had to make a choice to become Indonesian citizens or stay Dutch citizens. The ones who became Indonesian would be freed. The Dutch would stay in prison and would be transported to the allied troops in time. Most people kept their Dutch nationality. To my surprise, Victor signed to become Indonesian. Most of the Indos with Indonesian relatives chose to stay Dutch citizens. I asked Victor why he was doing this. He told me he had his reasons. "My father and my grandfather were born here, and so was I. This beautiful country is ours, I'm not willing to give it up," he said. I said, "You don't have to give it up." I told him when we get transported to the allied troops things would get better. Victor said, "Just think if the Indonesians get what they are fighting for, there would be a generation of Indos without a country. The Indonesians don't want them, and the Dutch have no room for them in Holland." I said, "You are all wrong, when we get to the allied troops we will fight with the help of the Dutch and Americans, and we will take our country back and teach the rebels a lesson." "The Dutch will never give Indonesia up," Victor said, and he ended up being right. When everything was sorted out the Indonesians gave everybody a chance to change their mind.

It was moving time again; we were transported by train. Men, women, children, old and young, were all mixed together and put in third-class railroad cars. I was not in the same car with my family, but I knew to sit by the door. I don't remember how long this trip was, but I think it took two days or longer. It was the same old thing to many people, and there was only one bathroom. This time, there were women and children; it was a mess. We were going toward a colder climate, so the train was not an oven. They gave us food and water.

We arrived at the prison camp at night. I was with my family again and a lot of other people. We were put in a big hall. My guess was it used to be a sports arena or concert hall. The next morning, we were assigned a place. It was a big house, but three families were in the house. The women and children were in a room, and the men slept in the living and dining rooms on the floor. There was no water or electricity in the house. It must have been an upscale white neighborhood before the war. This camp was the biggest of all the prison camps I had been in. It was part of the city. The Japanese had used it as their internment camp. It must have been a mixed camp for a long time because there were babies born in the camp.

All the men got their turn to get water for their house. Our house was on a hill and the closest water supply was about a mile away. There was enough storage for water at the house, but the trick was getting it. The men made a pushcart that could hold about eight to ten five-gallon cans. It took about half a day to fill the cart. One person could only fill one five-gallon can, and if he wanted more he had to go back to the end of the line. There was always a line 24/7. My group stood in line for water day and night. When we had enough water in storage, we took turns taking a bath. There was never an argument at the water supply. Everybody knew the rules, one can at the time. I met some older men at the water line who told me that they were in the camp for five years. First, with the Japanese and then the Indonesians. The Indonesians were not any better than the Japanese. There was a Catholic church outside camp. On Sundays they let people go to church.

There was an eruption of a mountain close by, and the ash rain was so thick that the sun could hardly shine through. It lasted for three days. Everybody was advised to stay indoors. In just one day our water supply ran low. We had to get water, so we put a wet rag over our nose and mouth and a bed sheet over the cans in the cart. Before we got home there was already ash in the water. Before the water went into the reservoir it went through another bed sheet.

One day, the planes came back and dropped food packages again. In front of our house was a playground. The planes used the playground for one of their targets. The planes dropped loads of boxes, but the people in the camp must have had this experience before. The boxes were collected and stored in a warehouse. In the excitement of collecting the packages some of us snatched a few and hid them somewhere. We hid ours under the house. The next day, there were so-called police going house to house looking for the hidden packages. They looked everywhere including our crawlspace and attic. They did not find ours. Every family got a number and the food was distributed accordingly.

The news in camp was that the Indonesians would soon start transporting some of the prisoners to the allied troops, in exchange for their war prisoners. My guess was there were thousands of people in our internment camp. All families had a number. When the day finally came, several people were chosen. The numbers were picked at random, so it was a waiting game. Our number came up; everybody was happy to leave camp. A train ride to freedom at last, but it turned out to be a train ride from hell. The babies and little children stayed with their mothers while the rest of us were put in the railroad cars at random. These third-class railroad cars were old and dirty. They put too many people in a wagon, so there was hardly any space to sit. The train left at night with the windows and doors closed while the outside daytime temperature was around one hundred degrees Fahrenheit. Many people got sick and it was coming out of both ends. Many of the sick were lying on the floor or leaning against each other on a bench. There was one restroom, but for most people it was impossible to get to. The smell in the train was so bad it would gag a maggot.

    I got my place by the door. When the doors opened to bring us food and water I slipped out and crawled under the train to get some fresh air and do my thing; the guards never stopped me. Sometimes they gave me extra water. This train ride took three nights and two days. Early on the morning of the third day, the train stopped, and the doors and windows opened. The ones who could get off the train by themselves walked on the railroad tracks across a river to where the allied soldiers were waiting for us. I don't know how the other people got across the river without help. I looked at the Indonesian captured soldiers, and they all looked healthy and well fed.

FREEDOM AT LAST

WE WERE LOADED IN trucks and transported to a military camp. We had to take our clothes off and clean up. Finally, a shower with real soap! We were waiting for the Red Cross and the military to check on the sick and determine who had to go to hospitals. While we were waiting, I smelled fresh baked bread. I went through a side door and came into a building with racks full of bread. I had never seen that much bread in one place. I took a loaf and started eating. A man, who I think was the baker, took the bread away from me. He said, "If you eat that loaf it could kill you." I asked if the bread was poisonous. He said, "No, your stomach will explode, now get out of here!" After the Red Cross had sorted everyone, they fed us, but made sure that we did not overeat.

With the families reunited we were transported to what I called Red Cross holding camps. Again, we had to share the housing with other families. My family had the front part of a house. Our neighbors were very friendly and had lived in the camp for a while. They instructed us about the rules in the camp. Anything was better than what we were used to. We slept in beds and cots with pillows under mosquito netting.

The next morning all the newcomers were gathered in a huge tent. We were served breakfast, oatmeal from what I remember. Then the party began! There were three smaller tents in a big tent. Before you went in the first tent you got a shot in the arm, I don't know what it was for. In the first tent you took your clothes off, then got a haircut, then you had to keep your eyes closed and hold your breath while they sprayed you with yellow powder. In the second tent they put you under the shower and scrubbed you clean. There were many women doing this; they were either nurses or doctors. In the third tent they took blood samples and checked you from top to toe. They went through everything, including the butthole! You came out of the third tent naked as a jaybird and got another shot in the butt.

Then you were measured for clothes and shoes. I had problems finding shoes to fit. I had been barefoot for a long time. I got shirts, boxer shorts, long pants, socks, shoes, toothpaste, a toothbrush, and a comb. Military stuff. Food and drinks were served, but they were limited for our own good. I got my physical report, and it said what I already knew: Malaria, beriberi, and bad teeth. It was all taken care of. The doctor told me the malaria would stay with me for life.

The first day walking with shoes was a problem for me. I overdid it and I got blisters on both my feet. The blisters were so bad that I had to let them heal before I could try shoes again. I got thicker socks and did not walk much. We got free passes to ride anywhere on the city bus. My friends and I picked a bus and rode it to the main station. We would pick another one and ride with the bus wherever it would go. We knew that all the buses came back to the main bus station, and we knew which one to take home. We had no money, and we carried a military canteen with water on our waistband. Sometimes, when we were tired, we sat against the wall of a Chinese restaurant and inhaled the nice aroma, drank some water and pretended we had eaten in the Chinese restaurant.

Every day there were husbands, fathers, looking for their families. There were happy reunions, but disappointments too. There were husbands with new families, and wives with babies from the Japanese. Some husbands took their family back with the Japanese kid. Others made sure that their family had housing and an income. My father had not showed up yet. Through the Red Cross my mother found out that he was back working for the railroad, and that he already had a new family. My mother did not want him back. All she wanted was housing and money to live on, but this took time. A sister of my mother who had a very small house with five people living in it told my mother that we could move in with them. Her husband did not come back from the war.

It was a mistake. The house had only one bedroom, one bathroom, and one restroom. With ten people living there it was a struggle to get a turn to use the facilities. At night, when all the cots were put in place, there was no room to walk, no mosquito netting, and the bedbugs were feasting on us. In hindsight, we would have been better off staying with the Red Cross. When my father showed up it was unpleasant to hear my parents fight. I thought my mother did not deserve it; she had gone through so much already. I told my father if he came here only to fight with my mother then he was not welcome.

My sister found a job at a beauty salon. I registered to go back to school. I was sent to a grade school close to my house. At the school there were many young men and girls between fourteen and eighteen wanting to get an education. The older boys and girls were separated from the grade school kids. We could not take any schoolbooks home. During school I asked where I could find work after school. One of the boys told me to go to the army motor pool because they always needed people to pump gasoline. He told me it would be hard work.

The motor pool was not too far away. I went there after school. I told the man in the office that I heard that he was hiring people to pump gasoline. The man asked how old I was, and I told him. The man said he was looking for bigger and stronger boys. I said, "I need work and I will keep up with anybody, just give me a chance." He said, "I'll give you a pass to go through the gate, but it is up to the man there." That man looked at me, and said, "You want to pump gasoline, do you know how?" I said, "I have never done it, but I could learn, and I will do anything you want me to do." He told me to go to gasoline pump number two, it was close to his office, and tell the men that I would be helping them pump gasoline.

The pump was a little tower with two glass bowls on top. It was a hand pump. When emptying one bowl you had to pump at the speed the other bowl was emptying. When you couldn't keep up you would have to prime the pump to get it going again, which meant lost time. It was a two-man job, but the man at the nozzle regulated the flow of the gasoline. Since I was new and did not know anything, the man I was working with let it flow full blast and I could not keep up. They had to prime the pump and said it was my fault. I said, "I pumped as fast as I could."

"Not fast enough," they said. I thought I had lost the job. The foreman knew what they had done. He scolded them and replaced them with two other boys. These boys were friendly and helped me. We pumped gasoline until the shift was over without any problems. The next day my arms were so sore I could hardly lift them. I even had problems holding my pencil.

At school the boy who told me about the job asked me if I got it. I told him I started pumping gasoline, and that I worked a full shift the day before. "How long do you think you will last?" "As long as they want me," I said. "It's hard work, you're lucky if you last three days," he said. The foreman let me work with the same two boys. We got along fine, and I never told them how sore I was. After about ten days I could pump gasoline and handle the nozzle with the best of them. There were three of us on a pump, two working and one off; we would rotate every hour. This was the first work I was being paid for. I felt like I was somebody. During the Japanese occupation I did a lot of hard work and never got paid for it. The only reward I got was being caned, kicked or slapped around.

The truck drivers didn't like waiting at the pump. They would park the trucks in line, then go to the canteen and have a beer. There was a lot of time lost. This was an opportunity for me to learn to drive. When I wasn't pumping gasoline, I would always climb in the cab with the driver and watch how it was done. Some of the drivers let me try, but I would either kill the engine or make the truck jump.

There was one driver who noticed that I was really trying to learn. He helped and told me that first I needed to find out where first gear and reverse were. He showed me, then he showed me the hand throttle and said, "You pull this knob and raise the RPM a little, then push the clutch pedal all the way in, then put the truck in gear, then let the clutch pedal up real slow. When the truck is moving, concentrate on where you are going, then push the clutch pedal in, and step on the brake pedal." Then he told me to take the truck out of gear and set the hand brake. With the help of the truck driver I got better by the day.

I was not handling the pump much anymore. The truck drivers were not waiting to get to the pump anymore. They knew that I would drive them to the pump and park the trucks. The drivers didn't like me adjusting the seat, but I couldn't reach the pedals. I carried an empty jerry can with me and put it behind me on the seat, which solved that problem. This went on for a while until one day I got called to the office. The first thing the man in the office said was, "Who gave you permission to drive the trucks?" I said, "Nobody, but we were losing so much time waiting for the drivers to finish their beer." "How did you learn to drive the trucks?" he asked. I said, "By watching and asking questions." He said, "I have to let you go." I thought I was fired. Then he said, "Be here at 8:00 tomorrow morning." I said, "I can't, I go to school in the morning until 1:00. "Then come right after school," he said.

In the office my boss gave me my money and introduced me to my driving instructor. The man looked at me and said, "You have to get more meat on those bones." I realized that I could become a truck driver. He took me to the military airbase and said, "Here is where you will learn how to drive." There were many young men who wanted to become truck drivers. First, we had to learn what made the truck work. Then we had to learn to check the engine, the oil, the tire pressure, the brake fluid, and other things. In class we had to read pages out of a book, and the instructor would test us on it. Finally came the hard part: we had to drive and shift on a simulator. There were no synchronized gears or automatic transmissions on our trucks. This was where many of us failed.

Once I mastered shifting on the simulator, the instructor let me drive his jeep to the field to check on the students who were taking the driving test. The day I got my military driver's license the instructor said, "I want you all to try this test." He showed a film clip with a truck on an uphill road. Then we saw him put matchboxes against the rear tires. The truck pulled up the hill and left the matchboxes behind. The instructor asked, "Did any of you see the difficulty in this test?" We all said, "No." "Are there any of you who want to try this test? If you pass, I will promote you to instructor," he added. We all tried, and all of us crushed the matchboxes. The instructor said, "You are all licensed truck drivers, but you still have a lot to learn."

At the motor pool the new drivers were assigned to an experienced driver. I was still in school, so I could only drive in the afternoon. I got lucky because my senior driver was the man who showed me how to move a truck my very first time. His job was to bring food to the soldiers at the outpost twice a day. It was dangerous to get to the outpost because you had to drive through rebel territory, and there was always a chance you would get shot at. The first few times he did not let me drive, but he explained everything he was doing. He was a very nice person. I noticed that there was always food leftover. I asked him if I could have some to take home. He told me to take all that I wanted. He asked me where I lived, and I told him. We dropped off the food at my house before going back to the motor pool. The next day he said, "Let's drop off some food at your place before we feed the soldiers." Before long he was satisfied with my driving, and I did most of the driving.

At school I made good progress and I made friends with my classmates. Two of my classmates introduced me to their friends. There were eight of us: four boys and four girls. We always met at this one girl's house. Her father did not come back from the war. Her mother liked us to meet at her place, and she took good care of us. There were always snacks and drinks. Sometimes we were invited to sleep over, and we would stay over from Friday night through Sunday. The girls slept in a room with the girl's mother, and the boys slept in the front room. It was always so much fun. We went to the swimming pool, the beach, or took long walks in the mountains. Her mother (we referred to her as our den mother) was always with us. I could not always participate in the outings because I had to work. The soldiers at the outpost had to be fed. Sometimes her mother checked on our schoolwork. Five of the kids in the group had never gone to internment camp and were much further ahead in their education than the three of us who were interned. They helped me a lot with my schoolwork and that was the reason that I did so well in class.

There was this Dutch girl, who was born in Holland, who liked me. We were always together, and she helped me with my schoolwork. Her parents were rich, but she liked to hang out with us. Sometimes she took all of us to the private yacht club her parents belonged to. Food and drinks were always on her. We went to the movies, soccer games, the yacht club and other functions together. We were always first class, and we would go in one of her parents' cars with a chauffeur. I was not romantically involved with her. I did not dare, and she trusted me.

The school year was over, and it was graduation time. I was in the top ten. The principal gave a speech. First, he talked about us boys and girls that did not go to school for a long time, and how well we caught up. But this was where the free education came to an end and we had to make room for others who were also behind. Then, he talked about the future. He told us higher education, trade school, military, or police were options we should look into. "I have the test papers in my office, and you can pick which test to take," he added. I took the college and trade school tests, and I passed both. The principal asked me which direction I wanted to go. I wanted to go to college. He said, "I advise you to go to trade school because it costs less, and it doesn't take that long." He showed me the cost of trade school. I could not afford it.

At home, I showed my mother my diploma and my test scores. She was very happy for me and said, "Now you can pursue your dreams." I showed her what it would cost to get me through school. She cried and said, "Maybe your father can help." I said, "Don't count on it; if he wanted to help, we would not be in this situation." My mother said, "I'm so tired of living in this crowded house." "So am I," I replied.

I went to the motor pool and told my boss that I was done with school and that I would like to start working full time. My boss told me he would try to get me more work. When there was work, I worked seven days a week. On the weekends I drove a bus at night with two MPs to pick up the GIs who missed the last city bus, but sometimes there was no work.

I went and visited my den mother. I told her that I could not continue my education. I asked her not to tell my friends since they were all in school. I told her that I would visit her more often during the day. When I had to work in the evenings, I missed out on the get-togethers at the den mother's house. In the meantime, my mother got things straightened out with the railroad. She got a big house and a pension. Things were looking up for her. I got my own bedroom.

One morning when I came to work, my boss asked me if I was interested in a job in the private sector. "What kind of a job?" I asked. He told me it was a better job and I would work five days a week from 7:00 a.m. to 4:00 p.m. I told him I didn't have my public driver's license. "You'll take the test," he said. "You know how corrupt the system is, I might have to take the test ten times before they pass me. Unless I come up with lots of money the first time, which I don't have," I replied. "You are a good driver, and I think you will pass the first time," he said. "Okay," I said, "I'll give it a try."

My boss introduced me to a Chinese man and said, "Here is your driver." The Chinese man said, "I hear you are a good driver." "I do my best, when do you want me to take my driving test?" I asked. He said, "You'll drive with me first, before you take the test." He took me to his motor pool. There were many trucks parked and ready to go. He said, "You see that blue truck there?" – it was a brand new 1948 Chevrolet flatbed. "That will be your truck, if you pass the test." He went in the truck. I walked around the truck and checked the tires, looked under the truck, opened the hood, checked the oil, water and other things. Finally, I went in the cab and pushed on the brake. "What are you doing?" he asked. I said, "At the motor pool where I work, we have to check everything before we take off, it's a habit." "I like that," he said. He told me to drive to a warehouse to get the truck loaded.

What a difference between his truck and the steel boxes the military had. After the truck was loaded, he told me to drive to the shipyard. At the shipyard he got a pass for us to get in, then he said to go to pier seven. After the truck was empty, we went to the parking lot. "Here," he said, "tomorrow when you come to work, you go from here to pier seven and you'll get your instructions there. By the way, how do you get to work?" "I get here by train, but it's a long walk to the shipyard," I said. He told me in the morning there would be a bus that would take me to my truck. Then he said, "Here is your pass; don't lose it. You can't get in without it." I said, "But you know that I have no public driver's license." He said, "Don't worry about it, and I have not told you what the pay is." He told me what my pay would be, and I was shocked. It was so much more than what I was used to. Then, he said, "If you drive for six weeks, and don't have a scratch on the truck, I will double your wages."

Before my probation time expired my boss had me take my driving test. With an empty flatbed and my boss present it was easy. I asked my boss if he knew if I passed or not. He said he didn't, but he would let me know. I very seldom saw the boss because I got my pay at pier seven. My next pay was unbelievable to me. I told my mother if I could keep the job for three years I could go to college. In those days we couldn't get an education first and pay later. As far as I was know, you couldn't buy anything on credit at this time.

One day before quitting time, the boss came over and inspected the truck. I asked him if he was satisfied. He told me I was taking good care of the truck. We talked some more, but then I saw people going to the bus. I told him I had to go, or I would miss the train. He said, "I'll take you home in the car." Then, he said, "Here is your driver's license." I asked, "How much do I owe you?" He replied, "It's a gift." "Where do you live?" he asked. I told him, and he laughed, "That is at the other end of the world." Then he asked me what time I had to leave my house in the morning. I told him it was very early. Then, he said, there are not many of you, meaning Indos, doing this kind of work. I told him that there would be many more soon. Then I told him about the Japanese and Indonesian internment camps and the lack of education we faced while in camp. At home I found out my driver's license was not only for driving trucks, but it was for all commercial vehicles.

Life was good. I spent a lot of time with my friends. I had a place to come home to, and my mother was happy again. This went on for some time. It was a very happy period, and this circle of friends felt like it would last forever. Then one day the Dutch girl told me her parents wanted to meet me. I said, "Okay, where do you live, and what time?" She said, "My chauffeur will pick us up here, the den mother's house, on Saturday at 3:00." My den mother said, "Put on your best clothes and shoes, her parents are very rich." Exactly at 3:00 the car picked us up. My den mother said, "Good luck and behave."

The house looked like a palace: an iron gate up front, a long driveway, covered swimming pool on the left, tennis court on the right, and a patio with a marble floor. It was all luxury in this house. I could not understand why this girl would hang out with us. I was not comfortable. After the formal greeting and a cup of tea we made small talk. Her father got up and asked me to come to his office. The first thing he asked me was what I was majoring in. I said, "I don't go to school, I work." He said, "My daughter likes you and I want the best for her." I did not answer. He asked, "What kind of work do you do?" I told him I drove a truck at the shipyard. In those days an Indo driving trucks was low class. I could see on his face that he did not like my answer. "That is no work for a young man like you," he said. "You have to get an education and become somebody," he added. I did not say anything, but I thought, "If he just knew how hard I was trying." He asked me if I got a pass to get in the shipyard. "Yes," I said. He asked to see it, and when I gave him the pass he wrote the numbers on a piece of paper and told me that would be all.

Back at the den mother's house, after the girl left, my den mother asked, "How did it go?" "Not good," I said. He talked to me in his office and wanted to know what I was doing with my life. I told him that I worked, and I am not going to school. He let me know that I did not measure up to his expectations, but he did not forbid me from seeing his daughter. The den mother asked, "What are you going to do?" "Nothing," I said. I didn't think that she knew that her father didn't like me. If she kept coming to my den mother's place, without acting differently, she would be my friend.

When I went to work the Monday after my meeting my boss was waiting for me at the railroad station. He did not look happy. I asked him, "What are you doing here so early?" He said, "Don't go on the bus, I have to talk with you. I have bad news and don't know how to begin." I said, "Did I do something wrong?" "Not by me," he said. "Yesterday, the top person of the shipyard summoned me to his house and showed me these numbers," he explained. Then, he added, "These numbers happen to be yours." He said, "If I don't get rid of you today, he is going to pull my contract, and all my trucks will be idle." I did not say anything, but things became clear to me. I told him that I knew who had done this, and I realized why he had asked for my pass numbers. He was punishing me. I said, "I understand, I'll take the next train home." My boss said, "I don't understand how you got mixed up with a person like him." "It is a long story, his daughter and I are friends, and he doesn't like it," I told him. I gave my pass to the boss. He gave me money and told me he was sorry.

I went to our den mother's house. Nobody was home, so I sat down on the porch and waited. She was surprised to see me and asked what happened. I told her the story. We talked some more. She said this girl is such a nice girl and she feels at home with us.

"I don't think that she knows that her father doesn't like you," my den mother added. "I don't know whether he likes me or not, but what he wants me to understand is that I'm not good enough for his daughter," I said. My den mother made lunch. Before I left, I told my den mother that I wouldn't be around for a few days; I had to let it all sink in. Then, I told her not to tell the girl anything about her father and me. I asked my den mother to watch whether the girl was acting any differently. "If she asks about me, tell her I lost my job and I am looking for another one," I said.

At home, I told my mother my college dream was over because they didn't need me at the shipyard anymore. She told me I would find another good job. I never told my mother about the Dutch girl. I stayed home for a few days and stayed in my room. My mother asked me why I was acting so strange. I told her I was reading books. I was debating if I should tell the girl the real reason why I lost my job at the shipyard. I made up my mind not to tell her. I decided it was her father's responsibility to tell her the truth.

School was almost out for the other kids, so we made plans for their vacation. Our den mother had trips scheduled. My two friends who had gone to the catch-up classes with me were homeschooled. They both had a complete family and their parents wanted them to catch up and go to college. I was the only friend who didn't have a job or go to school. I was still planning to spend the vacation with my friends. Shortly before vacation started, the Dutch girl came over crying and told us she had bad news. "I'm not spending the vacation with you guys, and I might never see you guys again," she said. "My parents are sending me back to Holland to finish school there," she added. "I don't know why, the schools here are just as good, and I can live at home. In Holland I'll have to go to boarding school. I tried to reason with my parents, but they have taken care of everything already. I'm leaving three days after school is out," she said. I knew the real reason, but I wasn't going to say anything to her.

Our den mother decided not to go on vacation until after she left. During the three days before she left, the Dutch girl spent most of her time with us. She cried a lot and didn't want me to leave her side. Everybody was planning to go to the harbor to say goodbye to her. I told her that I wouldn't be going with them. "Why won't you go?" she asked. I told her it hurt too much. The real reason was that I didn't want her father to see me. Now there were seven of us. I spent more time with the den mother. She took care of everything. I wasn't aware how much planning it took to get us on these outings. The vacation was fun. We did a lot of camping, hiking in the mountains and swimming.

After my friends went back to school, I had a long talk with my den mother. I said, "It's time for me to say goodbye; I have to find work." She replied, "When you're in the neighborhood drop by, you are always welcome." Good jobs were hard to find. Indonesia was taking over everything little by little. At the market where the truckers came to find work there were go-betweens: coyotes, scalpers, or whatever you call them. For me, it was difficult because I wasn't Indonesian, and I was new at this.

One day, I came home after an unsuccessful job hunt and there was an old friend of the family from before the war talking to my mother. After a formal greeting I asked him how his son was doing. His son had been my best friend when we were little kids. He said, "My son is in town taking a test to go into the Navy, the Dutch Navy." He said, "Your mother told me that you are on a dead end." I said, "I'm trying, nothing has worked out so far." He said, "The Navy needs more young men, and if you are interested, I will cover the expenses."

At the Navy office the doctor took my physical. I didn't pass because there was malaria in my blood. I didn't get to meet my friend because he passed and went to boot camp. I continued to live at home where my mother fed me and I had a place to sleep. I was frustrated; everything I tried did not work. There was always work for strong men at the railroad warehouse. They carried one-hundred-kilogram rice sacks from the railcar to the warehouse. I tried, but I could not carry the weight all day.

With nothing to do I watched the neighborhood soccer team practice. They invited me to play. They liked what they saw and invited me to join them. There were many soccer teams in the neighborhoods that we played against. One team member and I were asked if we would play with the big boys and get paid. I accepted, but my friend did not. I did not like the way they ran the players. One of the rules was if you could take out the best players on the opposing team you would get a bonus. I was a good runner, so when I stepped onto the field, I was a target. It did not take long before I got a knee injury, and somebody got a bonus. I played with an injury but had to give it up.

After I healed, I went back to the market trying to find a driving job. I was hired to haul wood coal for cooking. My truck was a 1941 Chevrolet truck without any doors, and you had to crank it to start. The coal factory was in rebel territory, so I had to make it out of there before dark. It was off the paved road. When it rained the dirt roads were slick, and it took longer to get back on the main road. I was lucky; I never ran into trouble. It was always a ten- to fourteen-hour workday. If you got lucky you could make three trips in seven days. My employer said, "From now on, I'll give you a bonus for every truckload you bring in." I asked, "Why the generosity?" He said, "No driver has lasted this long."

One day I was waiting at the truck stop for somebody I needed to take back to the coal factory when I saw a huge Army truck. I approached the driver, who was an Indo, and I asked him what he was doing there with an Army truck. He said, "The truck is mine and I'm looking for work." I said, "Give me your address and we'll talk when I get back." I went to the man's house and inspected the truck. It was in good shape; it was a military truck with big single wheels, and double axles high off the ground. It was perfect for what we needed, for going off the paved road. I asked the man how he was doing finding work for the truck. He told me not well. I said, "I know, as an Indo at the truck stop, you are always last in line." I told him my plan.

I told my employer that I had a bigger and more dependable truck. We agreed on the price and he guaranteed us that he would buy all the wood coal. I told my new friend that I made a deal with the man. Then I told him, "But, before I tell you where the coal factory is, I want to know what there is in it for me." He said, "I have a hard time finding work and I'll give you half of the profit." I said, "You made me your partner." He said, "You could say that." Then, I told him that the wood coal factory was in rebel territory, and that we would have to be on the main road before dark. He said, "You have made it, I'm willing."

The business went great. The Chinese businessman kept his word. He was getting rich, and we were making good money. There was always demand for wood coal. When the dessa villagers needed goods from the city we would get it for them. We wouldn't charge them for transportation and in turn they would give us discount for the wood coal. This was a win-win proposition. We started driving at night in the dry season. It made our business partner happy, and he always had a big smile on his face when we got to his place in the morning.

Sometimes we would haul raw rubber. It came in bales of one hundred kilograms. The rubber went to another Chinese businessman. The wood coal businessman found out and said we couldn't haul rubber anymore. We told him the pay was better, so he upped our pay, but we still hauled rubber. We made so much money that we were thinking of buying a second truck from the Dutch Army surplus. My partner was an ex-military man, so he got a big discount. It was almost the rainy season; we were driving day and night. Our greed was not rewarded.

One evening before we got to the paved road, the rebels ambushed us: guns drawn and aimed at our heads.

They wanted money. They said if we gave them all our money, they would let us go. I spoke their language. I told them they could have all the money we had, and we gave it them. The rebels were not happy with the amount. They looked everywhere in the truck but couldn't find any more money. Then they turned on us. They made us take off our clothes, and they took everything. They left us standing barefooted in our underpants. Finally, they set the truck on fire. We had two full tanks of gasoline, a load of raw rubber, and wood coal. It was a huge fire; nothing could be saved. I told the rebels if they would have let us go, we could have brought them money the next time. They told us to be thankful they did not kill us. There we sat in the night close to the big fire. The worst thing was we had all our money stashed away in a secret compartment welded to the body of the truck. Everything went up in flames; even the metal on the truck melted. Our hopes and future were destroyed.

We sat by the fire until daylight. In the distance we could hear the morning bus coming. We ran to the highway and from the middle of the road we waved it down. The bus driver picked us up. He asked, "Is that your truck burning there? "Yes," I replied. He said, "You know better than to drive through here at night." We got to town and went to the wood coal distributor first. He told us he knew that it was just a matter of time before this would happen. He gave us money and told us to buy some clothes and shoes, but other than that he showed no sympathy. We went to our raw rubber client. We told him the story. He said, "I'm so sorry, you are very lucky to be alive." I said, "That is true, but we lost everything, we are flat broke." He gave us money and said, "I wish you all the luck. You guys are hard workers."

I asked my partner if he would like to be a truck owner again. "What do you mean?" he asked. I said, "We could get back to work, put our money together, and you could buy another Army surplus truck." "No, thank you! This adventure will last me a lifetime," he said. I went home and told my mother that I was out of a job again. She said, "You must have made a lot of money; you were away for a long time." I said, "I have very little money, the truck caught fire and our money was in it." I never told my mother the real story. I didn't want her to worry.

I bought a bicycle. I went to visit my den mother, and she was happy to see me. She wanted to know how I was and what I was doing. I always told her the truth. She said, "You are lucky to be alive, but bad luck got you again." I asked her how the rest of the gang was doing. Some of them were thinking of going to Holland and continuing their education. The others were working in the city. Then she told me she got letters from the girl in Holland, and she always asked how I was doing. Then she gave me some letters to read. She said, "She doesn't talk much about her life in Holland. She only talks about the good times she had here and the boy she never will forget." I said, "Wish her well for me." My den mother said, "Why don't you write her a letter?" I said, "I won't do that, I want her to forget me."

I was not looking for work. I was still getting over my last experience. I was hanging out at the swimming pool and made some new friends. We went on long bicycle rides. Sometimes we went to the beach and stayed overnight. At the swimming pool I made friends with a man; he was a body builder with an upper body that any man would like to have. In the war he lost both his legs above the knee. It was a pleasure to talk to him. He was always in a good mood.

One day I came home from one of my bicycle trips and there was a man talking to my mother. My mother introduced us, and said, "Meet my brother." This man was my uncle that I had never met before. After a lot of small talk, he said, "Your mother told me that you have had a hard time keeping a job." I said, "The jobs just end, and I have no skills other than driving." He said, "You have to learn a trade. I work for a tin-mining firm. I'm head electrician and have worked for the company for over twenty-five years. It's on another island, but if you are interested, I could get you a job there." I said, "I don't want to go to another island when I don't know what my future is." My mother said, "You will learn a trade there and your uncle will take good care of you."

WORK EXPERIENCES

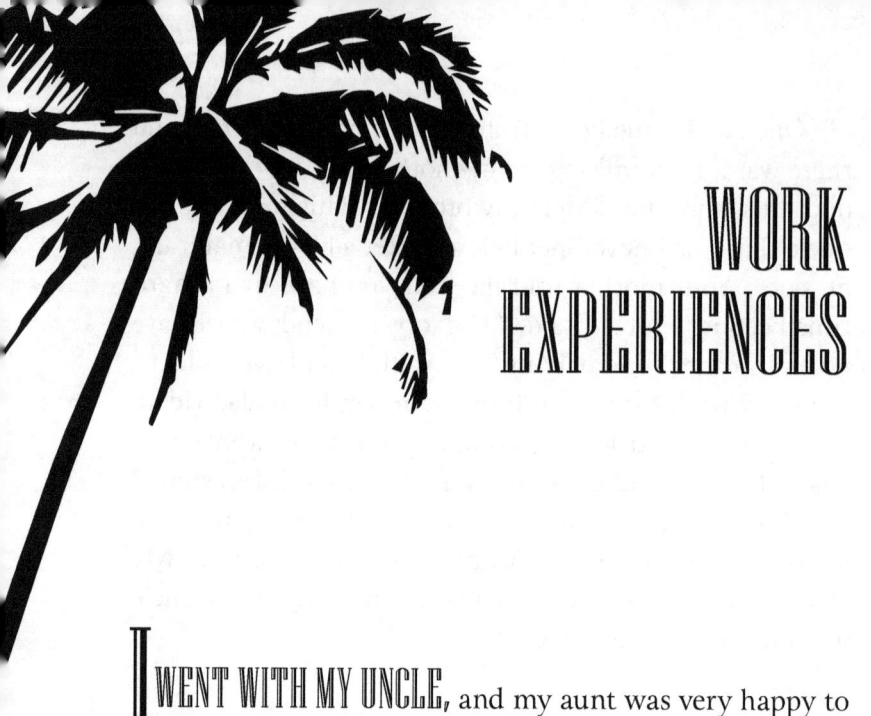

I WENT WITH MY UNCLE, and my aunt was very happy to have me because her three sons were on the main island of Java in school. My uncle put me to work. I did not like working with electricity. My uncle asked a friend to help. His friend put me to work with two diesel mechanics; both were Chinese and very hard to learn from. Most of the time I was cleaning parts, which was very boring work. The man who put me there saw that I was not getting anywhere. After work he was teaching me diesel motors out of the books he had. He was very strict, and I learned fast. I asked my uncle about my salary. He told me he was working on it, but for the time being I would be paid as a local. The starting wage was seventy-three cents an hour. I was not happy. He said, "You're learning a trade and we'll take care of you as our own son."

As a local, I did not have the privileges that the staff employees had. I could not go to the clubhouse and buy a drink, or go to the movies, swimming pool or anywhere else. The corporation owned everything. My uncle's card always solved the problem and he would take care of the bills. The corporation had everything brought in from the main island. Local fresh vegetables or meat was not always available. There was always plenty of fish, though. My uncle started a chicken farm. The local birds were small. He had his chickens imported. The chicken coops were first class; everything was automated. In the morning I had to check the water and feed the chickens. In the afternoon I collected the eggs. The staff employees were happy with the eggs my uncle sold them. My uncle designed and made his own incubators.

The first time the eggs hatched I had to watch to make sure things were going right. My uncle was very pleased with the process. He hired two locals to do the work and deliver the eggs. I had to fill the orders and check that the birds were taken care of. My aunt got sick and the doctor told her that she would be better off if she went to the mainland where the care was better. It was not the same without my aunt. Not long after that, my uncle put in for his retirement and sold the chicken farm. I asked him whether I would be a staff employee before he left. He said, "Your boss will handle it." I said, "I don't want to stay on the island if I'm not a staff employee." He said, "Be patient, things always take care of itself." My uncle retired.

As a non-staff employee, I could not keep the house. My boss moved into my uncle's house. He said I could stay until his wife came from Holland. This man wanted me to succeed, but he was very demanding, and he knew that I was available at any time. He taught me everything about how to keep the open pit tin mine running. There were three diesel engines in the mine that had to run day and night. One engine was for for electricity, a white diesel one for the water cannon, and a GM diesel one for the suction pump, which was a Caterpillar diesel. In the evening after dinner, he worked with me on how to keep the mine running. I got to know the diesel engines and could do minor repairs and maintenance. My boss gave me a pickup (staff employees already had this privilege) and had me run the mine. I also got a pager so that the telephone operator could reach me anytime.

There was a blond girl living next door. The first time I saw her I introduced myself; we talked for a while and I found out her mother was Swedish, and her father was Indo. She told me that she went to school in another district. On school days, she had to leave at 6:00 a.m. and wasn't back until 3:00 p.m. I told her that I was responsible for one of the mines and that I was on call 24/7. Whenever I saw her, I would wave or say hello. One day I came up the driveway and she was waiting for me. She said, "Why don't you like me?" I said, "I have no reason not to like you." "You never stop and talk to me," she said. I was thinking back; her parents might not like her being friends with me. I said, "I have a pager and when it goes off, I have to go to the mine." She asked, "What does that have to do with talking to me?" I had no answer. She said, "I go swimming from four p.m. to six p.m. When you have time, come over so that we can get to know each other."

I went in my house. There was my boss, with a grin on his face. He said, "What was that all about?" I said, "The neighbor girl wants me to go swimming with her." "And why are you here?" he asked. I said, "If I go swimming, I wouldn't hear my pager." He said, "Go! That girl needs somebody close to her age to be friends with and when the telephone operator can't reach you, he will get me." We became friends and spent a lot of time together. We had a lot of fun. However, it did not last. She was sent to Sweden to school. I missed her a lot.

Now I had to deal with adults all the time. The corporation bought three brand new bulldozers, and two Americans came to teach us how to run and maintain them. The bulldozers were used at the mine I was working at. The dozers became my responsibility. The funniest thing was that nobody spoke English, so the American instructors had a lot of fun explaining things. There were a lot of laughs. After I got the hang of running the dozers, I had to teach a crew. I loved operating the Cats. However, there was little time to do that because my boss made me run the mine. It was a big responsibility, but somehow my boss gave me a lot of overtime. It helped a little but compared to a staff employee with benefits I was only making about twenty-five percent of their income.

It was time for me to move out. My boss's wife arrived from Holland, and I had to find a place to live. The maid said, "There are empty rooms at the servant quarters, and I could take care of you." I didn't want to. I moved in with one of the Chinese mechanics. He was single and had plenty of room. An old Chinese woman took care of us, and I liked her cooking. The mechanic and I were seldom at the house at the same time. My boss didn't like this arrangement. He said I was hard to get ahold of. I moved back with him, but he did not want me to live in the servant quarters.

My boss's wife didn't like the island because there was nothing to do. They had no children and she did not drive. It drove my boss up the wall. He told me to stay at the house and take her wherever she wanted to go. The Chinese mechanic got my job. She made friends with the young women and they were on the go all the time. They had a lot of fun and their driver spoke Dutch. I didn't like it because there was so much waiting time. I told my boss. He said, "You don't like it? She drives me nuts!" My boss's wife went back to Holland. I got my job back. The Chinese mechanic was glad. He said the job had too many working hours.

My boss was transferred to another island, New Guinea, and wanted me to go with him as his assistant. He guaranteed that I would be a staff employee. According to the corporation I had to get permission from my father because I was not twenty-one. I never knew whether this was true. I came to the island without permission. My new boss had five children and he took the house. I moved back with the mechanic. After my new boss became familiar with the work schedule, he called me to his office. He said, "I see here that you are running a mine." I said, "Yes, I have been doing it for a year and have never had any trouble." He said, "That is work for an engineer."

Not long after that, I was called to the office and introduced to a young man. He was just out of engineering school in the Netherlands and didn't speak a word of Indonesian. My boss told me that he would take over my job at the mine, but that I would help until he got used to it. The next morning, I took the engineer to the mine and introduced him to all the foremen. I told them that they wouldn't be seeing me anymore. At the shop my boss said, "Give the keys to the truck and the supply records to him and be here in the morning at 7:00 a.m." I stopped showing up for work because I wanted to be fired. The telephone operator got ahold of me. He said, "I have been trying to get ahold of you for five days. The mine is running out of supplies, what is going on?" he asked. I said, "It is not my responsibility anymore, the company has hired an engineer. You have to get in touch with the man in charge."

On payday I showed up. I got a full week of pay without the overtime. It was not much; I could not live on my wages. I went to the top man of the district and complained. I said, "You knew what I was doing; now everything has been taken away from me. I can't live on the money, and I have no card to go to the company clubhouse or store." He said, "You have a new boss, and you have to go by his rules." "I don't want to work here anymore," I said. "Here is the problem, you were hired from the mainland, so only that office can fire you," he replied. I never knew if that was true. I didn't show up for work anymore.

The mechanic I was living with gave me the address of a wealthy Chinese businessman and told me the man was building a fishing fleet. He told me, "He is building a pier on the other side of the island and he needs a heavy equipment operator." I went to the man, and he hired me on the spot. He took me to the project. The man in charge of the work was an Indo. He was happy to have somebody to talk to in his own language. The labor force was Chinese. The pier was away from civilization; there was nothing there. There were a few small houses and a big barn-type building for the workers. Electricity was supplied by a generator, and fresh water from an underground well. I got one of the small houses. Chinese women took care of the meals and the housekeeping.

My boss did a lot of drawing. He oversaw the project. I worked all daylight hours. On rainy days, I did the maintenance and repair on the Cat. The pay was good. I was happy with my job, but it was quiet and lonesome at night. One morning a worker told me the boss wanted to see me in his office. I thought, "What could be wrong now, everything is going fine." In the office my boss told me there were two policemen that wanted to talk to me. They asked me a question, and I answered yes. They said I had to come back with them. I told my boss that I had to go with the police and that I might not come back. He asked me if I was being arrested. I said, "Kind of."

At the head office of the mining company they told me that if I was working for them, I could not work for anybody else. I said, "I quit, a long time ago." He said, "We have been over this before." I told him I had no place to live and I couldn't live on the pay I was getting. He said, "For the night you stay in our guesthouse, and I expect you to be at work in the morning." I went back to working with the diesel mechanics cleaning diesel engine parts. I told the mechanic my problem. He told me that there was a vacant house close to the warehouse. Then he added, "If they won't let you have that one you can come back and live with me." I said, "I could not pay you." He said, "I haven't charged you before."

I went to the head office and told them that I found a vacant house and where it was located. The man in the office told me that it was for staff employees only. I said, "I have to stay in the guesthouse and at my wages I can't pay rent." He said, "Find a place and maybe I can help." The next day I told them I found a place and what it cost. He gave me the money. I told the mechanic that I was moving in. At home I gave the mechanic the money. He asked me what it was for. I told him it was for rent money. "Why so much?" he asked. I said, "That is what I'm charging the company." He gave me an old bicycle to use. I was completely shut out from the staff privileges. I came and went as I pleased. The boss ignored me. I hated it. I wanted to get of the island.

Then one day I got called to the head office. I was sure I was being fired. Instead, they were making me a deal. A worker was injured and needed to return to the main island for surgery. I had to take him to the resort owned by the company, and they would take care of him from there. I told them that on the mainland I had no place to live and I would have no money. They told me that I could live at the resort at no charge for a month including meals. Before I left the mechanic gave me an envelope from my Chinese boss. He gave me some money and an address in case I ever wanted to come back.

On the mainland I had a place to live for free and money to spend. I was like a kid in a candy store. I knew that my mother had moved to another city. I went to my den mother and checked on my friends. She was very happy to see me. However, right away she said, "Did bad luck catch up with you again?" I told her the story. She said, "It must have been two years since I have seen you last." I said, "Enough about me, where can I find my old friends?" She told me I would have to go to the Netherlands to find them. I said, "What about your daughter?" She replied, "My daughter got married and went to the Netherlands with her husband." Then she added, "There is only one boy left; he works for the Dutch embassy. You could go and visit." I did, but he had little time to play around with me; he was getting his papers ready to leave.

My good time came to an end. I had to move out and my money was gone. I went to my den mother and told her that I could go back to the small island but that I didn't want to. The pay was good, and I could have a future there, but the loneliness was too much for me. She said, "You could live here with me as long as you want; I have plenty of room." I moved in with her. She took care of me, and never charged me.

Work was not easy to find. One day, I looked up my sister, whom I had not seen for a long time. She was married and had children. We had a lot to talk about. My sister told me that my neighbor had trucks and one of his drivers was sick. "Let's go see if he will let you fill in," she said. He hired me. I told him that I was new and did not know my way. He said, "Your helper has been on the route for a long time; he will guide you." The trip took four days. When I came back, his driver was well, and I was not needed any longer.

I told my den mother with the pay I got I was going home to see my mother. She told me that whenever I was in town I should come and see her. I promised that I would. I enjoyed being back at home. My mother took good care of me. My mother's sister was living in the same town, and she had a big house. It was a gathering place for young people. There was a park in front of the house. We spent a lot of time in the park playing soccer and other games. When we had money, we spent the day at the swimming pool. One of her sons had a good job. Sometimes he would take a group of us to the movies and pay for it.

One day, my father told me if I came to live with him, he would help me get an education. He lived a two-day train ride from where we lived. When I arrived at his place his wife had just had a new baby. I didn't get to meet her. My father showed me my room. It was in the servant quarters. The room had a place to put my clothes, a bed, a table, two chairs, and a pitcher of water with a glass. I didn't feel welcome.

The next morning, my father got me and told me it was time to meet the rest of the family. He introduced me to his wife. She said, "Now I'm your mother." I said, "I have only one mother." That did not sit well with her. She had two teenage girls and a nine-year-old boy. My father had two little girls, and together they had a baby. My father said, "You get acquainted with your new family, and this afternoon I'll introduce you to your teachers." His wife went back to the room with the baby, and the kids went to school. I spent the morning by myself. His wife never came out of her room. I had an uncomfortable feeling about this. However, the girls wanted to know everything about me, and they called me their big brother.

After supper, my father took me to meet my teachers. They were both retired and very nice. They told me to be there between 5:00 and 6:00 p.m. The next day, I asked my father, "How do I get there?" He said, "You walk." I said, "I'm new here, I don't know my way." My father drew me a map. I asked how long it would take me to walk there. He said, "If you walk fast, about one hour." I looked at him but did not want to say what I was thinking. The walk was all uphill. My teachers were surprised that my father made me walk. The lessons went fine, and they were very good teachers. I liked them. I asked them for lots of homework. In the morning I would do my homework until the girls were home from school. Then we would sit in front of the house and talk. Their mother didn't like them to be around me. She would always call them back in the house. I asked the girls why they never did things with kids their age. They said their mother wouldn't let them.

One day my father told me that I should find a job because doing nothing all day was not good. I said, "Where do I find work.?" He said, "I'll take you to town and I'll find you a job." I was hired at a car dealer where my father knew the owners. I was no mechanic, so I had to do the odd jobs: cleaning parts, washing cars, sweeping floors and what have you. Now I had a job and school in the evening. I spent one hour one way walking to work and one hour one way walking to school. I could not handle walking four hours a day for work and school.

One Saturday morning at breakfast, I told my father that I wanted to talk to him in private. His wife said, "If you have something to say, you say it in front of me." I looked at my father and he did not say anything. I began, "You promised me an education if I came to live with you. Now, I have to work and go to school. I spend four hours a day walking. There is no time to study. I can't handle it!" I told them. She said, "You're just a wimp, like your father." I said, "That is what I want to find out, do you ever make a decision?" I asked him. I went to my room.

Sunday night, I packed my belongings, what little there was of them, and went to my work place. The night watchman said, "You are a little early, aren't you?" I said, "I have no place to live. Could I sit here with you until you open the gate?" "And what is with the suitcase?" he asked. "Those are my belongings," I replied. He said, "It looks funny, you coming to work with a suitcase." I said, "I hoped you would open the gate, so I could hide my suitcase." He said, "I'll lose my job if I do that." Before daylight he unlocked the gate and let me hide my suitcase.

After work, I went to my teachers. I gave the books back and told them that I could not continue my lessons. They were sorry that it turned out poorly and wished me luck. Back at the car dealer, I told the night watchman that I would sit with him until he opened the gate each morning. He said, "You have no place to go home to and you want to sit here with me every night?" I said, "I have no choice, unless you let me in the shop; then I'll sleep in one of the vehicles." I told the night watchman that I had not taken a bath for days and my clothes were smelly. He said, "Don't complain to me."

The next evening, the night watchman gave me a bar of soap and told me to take a bath and wash my clothes. I was washing my clothes when one of the owners came in the shop and wanted to know what I was doing. I told him I was washing my clothes. He said, "The night watchman must have let you in." I said, "Please don't fire him, he is only helping me." He said, "After you're done washing your clothes, come to the office."

In the office, he wanted to know what really was going on. I told him everything and told him if he had to fire somebody it should be me. The boss then asked me what my plans were now that I was without a place to live. I said, "I would like to save money, and go home to live with my mother." He said, "I'm getting new vehicles from America, but they are being unloaded at the port in Djakarta and need to be driven up here. I'm looking for ten good drivers, are you willing.?" I replied, "Count me in." He told the night watchman to let me in the shop after hours. The company served lunch, and that was my only meal each day for quite a while.

When I was introduced to the drivers and the man in charge, I was happy to find out they were all Indos. The boss gave us the train tickets. We left early the next morning; it was a fourteen-hour train ride, a short rest, then a fourteen-hour drive home. This went on until all the vehicles were in. I was living in the shop again. I told the night watchman that I was thinking of going home after payday. That evening, the boss came to the shop and asked me to come to his office. He asked me if I was going home. I said, "Yes, I can't live on the money I am making." He said, "There is a trucking company in town who bought most of the trucks and they are looking for drivers." He added, "They have asked me if I know any. I thought you might be interested because the pay is very good." I said, "I'm very interested, thank you." He said, "Grab your suitcase, I'll take you up there."

The man who interviewed me was Chinese. He said, "We are a big corporation; We have offices in Djakarta, Semarang, Surabaya, and many offices in between." He said, "There are many unsafe routes for truckers." I replied, "Yes, mainly at night." "You have experience with that?" he asked. I said, "Yes, I owned a truck once, and the rebels set it on fire." He said, "When can you start?" I told him anytime. He left his office to talk to my boss. When he came back, he said, "I'll take you to the motor pool."

At the motor pool, he introduced me to the manager, who was also Chinese. He said, "I hired a driver." Then they talked away from me for a while. When the manager came back, he said, "I understand you are an experienced driver." I said, "Yes, but I did my driving in the west." He asked, "You have no home address here?" "I could live in the truck, I'm on the road most of the time anyway." He said, "No, I want you here until you know the company's rules and have learned your way in town." Then, he added, "I have rooms at the motor pool, but they are for truckers who only stay for a short time. I'll give you one, but you are responsible for keeping it clean and locked up." It was a small room; it had a bed and storage place. There was a public bathroom and washroom.

Then I was assigned to a truck and had to deliver some goods. My boss gave me one of the new trucks. My helper was very good, and he knew his way around town.

At the end of the day my helper told me where I could get good and cheap food. Then, he told me to have a good rest because we had a full day the next day. I asked, "How do you know what we have to do tomorrow?" He said, "It is on the board in the office." "What time do we have to start in the morning?" I asked. "Any time after 6:00 a.m.," he said. "How about 7:00 a.m.?" I asked. He said, "I'll be waiting for you." Then I told him that I didn't have a clock, so if I was late to knock on my door. He knocked on my door at 6:30 a.m. and took me to a place to have breakfast. Most days we worked ten to twelve hours, which the boss liked. I got along well with my helper.

One day we were hauling fruit from the railroad station, and I told my helper I used to live in the area. My helper asked if I knew the name of the street. I told him. He said, "That is close by." "You mind if we drive by?" I asked. I stopped in front of the house and the kids were out front. The girls saw me and came running. They were happy to see me. I gave them a basket of fruit. Their mother saw the girls talking to me and called them into the house. I never saw them again.

The other truckers were not as friendly. I asked my helper what I could do to become friends with them. He said, "Don't mind them; I'll make sure that your truck is in good condition." I said, "You are not telling me why they don't like me." He said, "You want to know so I will tell you. It is because you're not Indonesian and because I'm helping you, they don't like me either, but we will make it. I already told the boss when you get transferred to another truck, I'll go with you," he added. The boss knew about the truckers. I told him I appreciated it but asked why he would want to stay with me. He said, "I have worked with other truckers and they are not nice to work with, and they don't share their bonus money." I had to have eyes in the back of my head knowing how the other truckers felt about me.

One day, I was helping put a tarp on the truck when my helper came up from behind. I let him have it. He said, "You are dangerous." I said, "Do not sneak up on me." He was surprised and asked me how I knew Pentjak. I told him I had some training. He told me that every evening in the kampong village the men worked out. I asked him to take me there, but to find out if I was welcome. After work, my helper introduced me to the Pentjak players. They were friendly. I asked them if I could watch them work out.

The older guru sat with me and wanted to know what style of Pentjak I played. I came from the west, so I didn't have much high kicking or jumping. The guru said, "Let's go in the ring and find out how well your style does against ours." I told him I would not spar against him because it was not respectful. He asked me to step in the ring and spar with his students. My helper said, "You are going to be floored." However, I held my own against his students. The guru told me to come back and that I was welcome to work out with them. My helper told me I was good, but I didn't want to talk about it. I worked out regularly. I incorporated Judo in my style. The players in the village were not comfortable being close, which helped me. The guru asked me to teach him some of the moves. I said, "Only if you give me some of your secrets." It worked well, and they incorporated some of my moves into their fighting style.

Word got around about the Indo who knew how to fight. At the truck stop many people were talking about it. The company hired a new driver. He was a big man and let everybody know not to mess with him. He was very pushy, and everything had to go his way. One day, I came to the truck stop to eat. It was crowded, but some of the truckers made room for me to sit down. The big guy said, "Why do you let this guy push you around?" The truckers answered, "Because we don't want to mess with him." He said, "How good could he be, he is just a little guy."

Sam told me once when I was little, "When you know how to fight, you will be challenged." The big guy came over, but before he could grab me, I grabbed two of his fingers, ducked under his hand, and twisted hard. He landed on the ground and I put my foot on his face and asked him what he wanted. He said, "Have mercy, I'm in pain." I let go, but I broke his fingers. I made him sit down and told him not to leave before he paid for the damage. The woman who ran the truck stop said in all the years she had run the business nothing like this had ever happened. I apologized but told her I had to defend myself. The man with the broken fingers was not fired. Whenever I came to eat there was always room for me.

In the kampong the guru said, "You are something else." I said, "Surprise is always better than to find out how good a person is." I got called to the office; my boss said you have been here long enough, it is time for you to move on. I said, "Are you firing me?" "No," he said, "I'm sending you to Djakarta, they need somebody like you." I asked, "What do you mean, somebody like me?" He said, "The company got a construction job and need men who are willing to work long hours." He said, "You are leaving tomorrow morning. Don't drive at night, here is your pay."

I went to my room to pack when my helper came in. He told me he was coming with me. He let me know he would take care of everything and the truck would be ready for the trip. I asked him what time in the morning we would have to leave. He told me we could leave by 5:00 a.m. I said, "Wake me up at 4:00 a.m. We went to the truck stop, had breakfast and left before 5:00 a.m. At 6:00 a.m. I asked him if we needed to stop so he could pray. He said, "When I'm with you, I pray in silence." In other words, he told me not to bother. I stopped to fill up the truck. My helper said, "I have packed some food, coffee and water. We could eat here, then you can drive until dark." Then he told me there were fish farms along the highway with little buildings built over them for traveling people to make pit stops. It got dark on us about two hours from Djakarta.

I got a room at the truck stop. After we ate, my helper went back to the truck to sleep. At these truck stops, there were men who guarded your truck. If you didn't hire them your truck would be sabotaged. All truckers gave them the going price. I got to the motor pool in Djakarta in the morning. The Chinese motor pool manager checked my papers and the truck. He told me to take the rest of the day off, and to be back at 7:00 the next morning. I asked my helper, "Where are we going to stay tonight?" He said, "I'll get a room here." "I'll stay with you for tonight," I replied.

I told my helper that I knew friends who lived in this town. I cleaned up a little and tried to find them. I went to my den mother's house, but she was not living there anymore. I asked the new people, they were Indonesians, whether they knew where she moved to, but they did not know. I went to my sister's house. The people there said my sister and her family moved to another island. I went back to the motor pool, and my helper noticed that I was back early. I said, "The people I know don't live here anymore. Let's get something to eat, then we'll go hang out in town." My helper said, "I'll go eat with you, but I'm not going to town with you." I went to places in town where I knew many Dutch and Indos hung out. I asked around about my friends and family, and the people in town told me that many Dutch and Indos moved away to the Netherlands.

Back at the motor pool, my helper warned me that I would be disappointed with the truck tomorrow. I said, "Let's not worry about it." In the morning, the manager gave me instructions on where to go and showed me the truck. The truck was an Army surplus truck with the engine in the cab; for ventilation of the engine they took the cover off. With the windshield propped open and the windows down, it still was as hot as an oven in the cab. It was a dump truck. I had to haul sand and mud for the tile factory.

The sand was taken out of the river without any equipment. It was scooped out of the river with a specially made basket, then dumped on the riverbank where a truck could get to it. Sometimes the men had to dive to get to the sand. Loading the truck was done by manpower. They carried the sand in baskets and dumped it in the truck. They would get paid by the basket. My helper counted the baskets and at the end of the day he compared the amount with the man in charge. They never had the same numbers, and they would always argue about it. The man in charge of the sand always had a much higher number than my helper.

I got tired of the discrepancies, so the next morning at the first load I told the man in charge we would compare numbers right away. It was already way off. I told him I was not paying him for his count, but I would pay him for the numbers my helper had. He said, "If you don't pay me for my count you have to unload the truck." I called his bluff and asked him where he wanted me to put the sand. He said, "Right back on the pile." I told my helper to stand where he wanted the sand and direct me to it. The man did not know that I had a dump truck. Before I left, I said, "You don't get paid," as we took off.

I went back to the shop and told my boss what happened. He was not happy with me. He said, "I should have made that decision." I said, "We gave you the numbers every evening, and you never did anything about it. If you wanted to pay what they charge, why did you have us count the baskets?" I asked. "I don't like working with dishonest people," I added. He said, "Where are we going to get the sand now?" I said, "Let me go back there tomorrow, and see if I can make a deal."

I parked the truck up the hill from where they were hauling sand. A man approached me and told me he would sell me sand, but it would cost more. We came to an agreement. I told him I would only pay for what I counted. At the end of the day there were only small differences. My boss was happy, and I got plenty of sand for the factory. We continued to work long hours. We always got back to the motor pool after dark. One evening there was a note on my door that the boss wanted to see me in the morning. My boss told me he wanted me to start hauling roofing tiles to the construction jobs because I could get them at the same factory. The Chinese man in charge was very friendly, and he said, "You bring the tiles to the construction jobs, and I'll take care of the rest." My helper went to the office to get the papers.

One day, I was watching the men loading the truck when a young woman walked up to me and asked if I remembered her. I gave her a blank stare. She said, "You must know me." I said, "I wish I did." She told me who she was, and I still didn't remember. She told me as kids we went to the same school, and as a matter of fact we were in the same class every year. She asked me to have lunch in hopes that it would jog my memory. I told my helper I would be back, and she went to get her car. "What kind of food do you like?" she asked. "Chinese," I replied. She looked at me and smiled. She was Chinese. I said, "I like you too."

At the restaurant, everybody did their best to please her. She ordered, then said, "Now, let's talk. You know the little Chinese girl who always got teased, the one you would walk home after school? You were my hero. I never thought we would meet again." I said, "You're beautiful." She said, "I would like to see you again. Tomorrow is Saturday, we can spend the day together." I said, "I have to check my schedule." She said, "Don't worry about your schedule, meet me at the coffee shop at 8:00 a.m. tomorrow."

At the truck stop my helper asked, "Do you know the girl you went out with today?" I said, "A long time ago, when we were kids, we went to the same school." "That is not what I meant," he said. "You hit the jackpot," he added. I asked him to explain. He said, "She belongs to a very rich family; her father owns the tile factory and many other businesses including the trucking firm you work for." I said to myself, "Here I go again, another rich girl." We spent a lot of time together. Whenever we went somewhere, she was treated like a celebrity. Once I knew where she was coming from, I played the game and wondered how long it would last. I was in heaven; we had a great time together.

I was called to the office and given orders to deliver building material to the motor pool in the east. It was a five-day journey. It took two days to load the truck and trailer. I told the girl that I had to leave and didn't know when I would be back. She was not happy; she said, "Tomorrow is Saturday; we could spend the day together." I said, "I have to get the truck ready to leave early Sunday morning." She told me she could put a stop to it. I said, "I don't work for you, I work for the trucking company." I was hoping that she would tell me that her father owned the company, but she didn't. On Saturday, we met at the coffee shop and she drove to a place where we watched the city lights and talked about old times. At about 10:00 p.m. I asked her to take me back to the coffee shop. She drove right to my front door. She knew all along where I lived. She kissed me and told me to hurry back and she would be waiting.

The truck was another Army surplus truck, a flat nose with the engine in the cab. I knew it would be a hot ride with the daytime temperature nearing one hundred degrees Fahrenheit. Since I was pulling a trailer, I got an extra helper, but there was no room in the cab for him. I said, "I just hope that it doesn't rain." He said, "Don't worry, I made myself a nice place under the tarp." The roads were narrow, and beside cars and trucks there were ox, horse-drawn carts, bicycles with all kinds of merchandise on them, men with yokes carrying heavy loads, women with baskets on their heads and a baby on their backs. Then there was me with a huge truck and trailer. It was slow going. I could only use second and third gear. I delivered the building material to the motor pool and expected to go back to Djakarta. Instead, they needed me there, so they gave me a room at the motor pool. I made many day and overnight trips.

After two weeks I asked the manager when he would send me back to Djakarta. He told me it would be soon, but instead I was sent back to the place where I was hired years earlier. The person who hired me was still in the head office. I asked him what the deal was. He said, "I need you; I have a contract with the British-American Tobacco Corp. I want you in the office at 7:00 a.m." The next morning, there were other drivers in the office who were mostly Chinese, one Indonesian and me. The boss said, "From now on you are hauling tobacco and cigarettes. There are many unsafe routes, and I don't want the word to spread." I made many trips from warehouse to warehouse in different cities.

One day, I had to deliver a load of cigarettes to a big city. I had to drive a full day through rebel territory. My boss said, "Be careful, don't stop, and take food and water with you." It was a nice sunny morning; before we hit rebel country, we rested a bit at the last safe truck stop. We bought some snacks for the long haul. It would be ten hours nonstop. We made good time, there was not much traffic and the scenery was beautiful. There were rice fields as far as you could see with mountains behind them. It made me sad to think that someday the Indos would have no country. The Dutch went home, and the Indonesians didn't like us. I was a third generation born in Indonesia but brought up and educated Dutch. My helper asked, "Why are you so quiet?" I said, "Because I can't sing," We both laughed. He gave me a snack and something to drink.

We were about halfway when the truck started acting up and quit on me. We had to wait for the engine to cool off before we could check what was wrong. A lone trucker came along and asked if we needed help. I said, "The engine is still too hot to work on." He said, "You better make it out of here before nightfall." The first thing that went through my mind was if there was water in the fuel we were doomed. I loosened the fuel lines and there was no water. I checked the vacuum hoses, and they were all in good shape. We were losing precious time and we couldn't find what was wrong. Of course, in those days we didn't have a cell phone. I said, "The last thing I can check are the spark plugs and ignition points." I was taking off the distributor cap when my hand touched the coil wire, it came loose and I fastened it. Thankfully, the truck started in an instant. However, the sun was going down and we still had five more hours to drive.

We ate the leftover food and decided that there was no other way than to keep on going. We came to the last mountain pass. We had another hour to go, and we could see the city lights in the distance. Then it happened: a bright light in the middle of the road shining at us. I stopped. Men with firearms surrounded the truck and asked me what I had on the truck. I told them just cigarettes. One of the rebels told my helper to get out of the cab and told him to go to the back of the truck. I expected him to be killed, and then it would be my turn, but I didn't hear any shots. I could hear them talking. Then he told me to take my shoes off, tied me to the seat with my hands behind my back, and blindfolded me. I could hear them removing the barricade and driving past it toward the city. Then they went down a side road that was not a paved road. It was a very bumpy ride that lasted about four hours.

When they finally stopped, they untied me and told me to get out of the cab. I was stiff as a board. I expected to be handled like the Japanese used to treat us. These men did not, they put us in a cage with a bench to lay on and a tarp over it to shield us from the rain and wind. In the cage my helper said, "How can you stay so calm?

I'm shaking, I'm scared!" I said, "If they are going to kill us, I'm not going to ask for mercy. I'm going with a clear mind. Now let's get some sleep. There are still a few hours before daylight." I went to sleep.

At daylight, the men came back with their faces covered and told us if we needed to go to the bathroom, we had to do it now. They gave us food and water and left. I did not know where we were. It was a wooded area somewhere in the mountains. I could hear children but couldn't see any houses. My helper said, "I know for a fact that every hijacked rig and crew have never come back." I said, "I know, but I never will show that I'm scared." In the evening the men came back and let us go to the bathroom again.

Before I went back in the cage the man said the chief wanted to see me. He blindfolded me, put a rope around my neck, and said follow me. I ended up in a room with a very bright light shining on me, so I knew they had electricity. There was a person sitting behind the light, but I could not see him. He told me to sit down. There was a moment of silence. He said, "You know better than to drive through here at night." I said, "My truck broke down, I had no other choice." He asked me many questions about my childhood: where I went to school, church, boy scouts, soccer, and many other things. He said, "It is you!" He turned the light off and said, "Come up here."

When I saw who it was, I could not believe my eyes, it was Victor! He said, "We have a lot to talk about." He said, "Tell me what you have done with your life since I saw you last." I said, "Not much, after Indonesian camp I went back to the real world. My parents split up, I tried to go back to school, but could not pay for it. I ended up working for the Dutch Army motor pool and learned to drive. Now, I am here as your prisoner." He said, "That is enough." Then he had me locked up in my cage. When I came back in, my helper asked, "What did they do to you?" I said, "Nothing, we talked." He said, "Why don't they just kill us now? I'm going crazy in this cage." I said, "Have patience, I'm trying to save our lives."

That evening, somebody took me to the house blindfolded and on a rope. Victor was waiting for me. He said, "Let's talk as friends, about old times." I said, "Okay, as a friend, how did you end up out here?" He said, "After I left internment camp, I joined the Indonesian Army as an officer, but the system is corrupt. I did not play the game and ended up fighting the government." He said, "That is enough, let's talk about old times." The nightly visits lasted for five days. I told him I met a girl in Djakarta that he would know. I told him about the little Chinese girl who always got teased at school. He said, "Nancy? The one you walked home every day." I said, "I had to go that direction." He said, "She had a crush on you." "I did not know, but you should see her now. She is beautiful," I replied. "I've spent a lot of time with her, and I think she has feelings for me, but she is out of reach for me," I said. He said, "Not if she is single." I said, "She is, but she belongs to a very rich family, as a matter of fact the trucking company I work for is hers." We talked until late in the night.

I asked him what his plan was for us. He said, "I'll let you know tomorrow evening." In the cage my helper asked, "Why are they torturing us like this?" I said, "They have done nothing to us, and we are going home soon." He said, "We are dead soon." I said, "Trust me, I'm working on it." That evening, Victor had dinner ready, a very good one at that. He said, "Have dinner with me, this is your last meal." I was thinking this could be the end for me and my helper, but then Victor said, "Let's talk about the good times we had as kids." At the end of our conversation he said, "Tonight somebody will drive you back to the main road, and the bus will take you to town." We shook hands. He said, "As a friend I'll never forget you." Then, he gave me a black headband with yellow lightning figures on it. He told me to wear it whenever I drove through rebel country, and it might save my life. I had tears in my eyes; I knew how hard it was for him to do this.

Back in the cage, I saw that they brought my helper food, but he had not eaten anything. I said, "Why are you not eating the food?" He said, "It might be poisoned." I said, "You should eat, otherwise you'll die from hunger, and if the food is poisoned, they save themselves a bullet." Around midnight, the men came with their faces covered like they always were, and they gave us our stuff back. I put my shoes on. They blindfolded us, put a rope around our necks, and made us follow them. It was difficult for us to walk. They tied me to the seat, and they put my helper in the back for the long ride to the main road.

At the main road, they moved the truck so we could not see it. They took the blindfolds off and told us the bus would be coming soon. We were standing in the middle of the road waving at the bus to stop. It looked like he was not going to stop, so we made it so he had to run us over if he didn't. When we got in the bus, the driver said I know you. I said, "Good, take us to town; I have no money." The bus driver let us off right at the motor pool. I told my helper to come with me to the office.

In the office, the manager looked at us like we were ghosts. He said, "How did you get here?" I said, "By bus and I'm sorry they stole your truck." Then he told us that everyone thought we were dead, and it even made the paper. "Stay there, I'll call headquarters," he added. "Now, tell me how you got out alive," he said. My helper said, "He is fearless, he went to their chief every night." I said, "I was summoned, and it took a lot of work to get freed." My helper added, "I still don't understand how he did it." I said to my helper, "You wanted to die, and I did not." The manager asked if they captured us during the daytime. I said, "No, the truck broke down, and it took us a long time to find the problem." I told him that it was actually a very simple thing. I told him how I checked everything then I found a loose coil wire, but by that time we had lost so much time that we could not make it out of there before nightfall. At the head office, they questioned us some more, then the boss told us we were the first on record to come out alive. He told us to take a few days off with pay. I said, "I don't need any days off, I'm ready to go on the road again." He said, "You'll go to Djakarta with a load of cigarettes." I looked at my helper and said, "If you want off, I could take somebody else with me." He said, "I'll go."

In Djakarta, I asked the motor pool manager for some time off. He said, "You earned it, let me know when you are ready to go again." I went to Nancy's work, but she was not there. I asked if anybody knew where she was. They told me she did not work there anymore. I asked if anybody knew where I could find her, but no one would give me a straight answer. I asked the motor pool manager if he knew where Nancy went. He said, "She got married and moved away." I knew for a fact that the Chinese would marry their children off against their will.

I told the manager that I was ready to drive again and that I preferred the long hauls. One day, I was on my way to Djakarta on a route that I seldom took. It was early in the morning, as a matter of fact, it was still dark when I saw a lot of smoke in the distance. It was one of our trucks on fire. I stopped, which was not a very smart thing to do. The people standing by the truck were not rebels; these were villagers who just got robbed. I asked the men standing around the fire what happened. They said, "First, they robbed us, then they attacked the truck, they killed the driver, took what they want and left." I asked, "Where is his helper?" They did not know. I wrapped the driver in a tarp and told the villagers they could keep whatever they could salvage. This was normally a safe route. I dropped the remains of the driver at the next motor pool.

In Djakarta, I was called to the main office. The boss asked me why I stopped. I told him that it was one of our trucks burning and I wanted to help. I did what I could. The boss said, "How did you know that the people were not rebels?" I said I didn't know. The boss said, "You are a brave man. The remains of the driver you saved was a family member of this corporation." Then the boss said, "You like the long hauls." I said, "The longer the better." He showed me a map with many little dots on it. He told me that all the dots were the stations I would have to go to, and where I would get my orders. He told me it would take a long time to cover them all. I asked my helper, "Are you willing?" He said, "I go where you go."

In the safe areas I would drive at night or early in the morning to avoid the traffic and the heat. I was driving at night on what was supposed to be a safe route. In the distance I saw smoke. I said to my helper, "It could be a truck burning there." He said, "I hope that we are lucky." I drove by, but there was nothing on the road. In the morning at the motor pool I asked what happened to that burning truck. They said it got ambushed during the daytime, but the rebels did not kill the driver. We drove for some time without any problems.

One early morning, we got stopped at an Indonesian military post. The commander told me to park my truck at the post. He said all traffic would be stopped. Further down the road there was a battle going on between the rebels and the soldiers. He didn't know when it would be safe again. Since I was the first one coming down the road, I could park at the post, but all the other traffic had to stay on the road.

The officer in charge asked me to come to his office. We talked about a lot of things. He was Indonesian, but Dutch educated. He asked me if I was on the road all the time. I showed him the map with the towns I had to go to and where I had been. He said, "Don't you have a place you call home?" I said, "I live with my mother, but my routes don't take me there." He asked if I ever had any problems with the rebels. I said, "Twice. The first time it was my own rig, and after they took what they wanted they set the rig on fire. The second time, it was a truck from this company; they kept me and my helper in a cage for six days blindfolded." "And you still drive day and night through rebel country?" he asked. I said, "I have no choice, driving is my life."

He said, "You must be tired. I'll tell my men to bring you a cot so you can rest." They brought me a cot complete with mosquito netting. I slept through the day and night. The next morning, they woke me up. The officer said, "I thought you were dead." I said, "I haven't slept this good for a long time." It took another two days before it was safe for us to leave. I was well rested. I gave the officer twelve cartons of cigarettes. He said, "My men will remember you."

I went through a long period of safe driving while visiting big and small towns. We were on our way back to the motor pool where I was first hired. Everything went fine and we were on schedule, but I was not feeling good. I was feverish; I had chills and a headache. We were about one hour from the motor pool when everything went wrong. I don't remember anything, but I woke up in a hospital in Semarang. I asked the doctor what happened. He said, "You had a severe malaria attack." "Where is my truck?" I asked. He said, "Everything is taken care of. You are not in good enough shape to do anything for a while." Then he added, "It took us three days to get you back. You will be staying in the hospital on medicine." I was very fortunate to be working for a big and rich corporation.

The day the hospital released me I was sitting in the waiting room not knowing where to go. There was this well-dressed lady talking to the doctor looking in my direction. She came over and said, "You come with me." I did not know her. I had never seen her before. I had no place to go, so I did not object. She took me in her car, which was chauffeur driven, to a big house. There was a small house in the backyard. She said, "Here is where you'll be living until you are well; let me show you the house." It had everything, including a refrigerator. She said, "You have a maid who does all the household chores including cooking your meals and washing your clothes."

The next morning, the lady had breakfast with me in my house. She said, "There are a few things you can't do. You can't go out on your own and you can't go in the big house." I didn't question her. I respected her wishes; after all, she was taking care of me. After breakfast, she said,

"I'll take you to town and buy you clothes." She bought me a lot of stuff. Many clothes and shoes that I wouldn't normally wear. Back at the house, she said, "Let's try on some of the clothes." I did not know how to put on a tie. She said, "I want you to wear these clothes tonight when I take you out to dinner, and from now on you call me Daisy." I was very uncomfortable. I never had a pampered life like this. She took me to fancy places. She would always introduce me as her son. I asked her why she did that. She said, "As long as you are with me, you are my son." I got tired of this lifestyle. There was nothing to do but listen to the radio and read books. Sometimes Daisy was gone for days and I had nothing to do. I asked the maid what was in the big house and why I couldn't go there. She said, "You don't want to know." Forget about the big house; otherwise you will be in big trouble." Eventually, she told me it was a house of pleasure.

I had to see the doctor two times a week and take my malaria medicine three times a day. Every time I saw the doctor, he gave me a shot. I asked him what the shot was for. He said, "They are vitamin shots to get your strength back." I told Daisy I was ready to go back to work. She said, "Not until the doctor says so, and I would like to keep you as long as possible." I said, "But you spent so much money on me, and I can never repay you." She said, "Don't worry about what I spend, you turned out to be such a good person. You deserve better, but I know you feel like a wild bird in a cage."

The day came that I could go back to work. Daisy came to the house. She was crying; she held me in her arms and kissed me. "Why are you so emotional?" I asked. She said, "If my son was alive today, he would be your age. He did the same work you do, but the rebels killed him, and we never found his body." Then it became clear to me how a mother felt when her son was away from home. She said, "Here is your suitcase; take the clothes and everything with you, and remember that I will always be here for you."

I went to the motor pool and everybody was happy to see me healthy. The manager asked me to talk in his office. I asked the manager how I ended up in the hospital. He said, "With the help of the police your helper got you to the hospital. Then he drove the truck up here and told me." He added, "When I got to the hospital, the doctor told me that you might not make it, but the rest is history." I said, "What about the bills, and the lady who took care of me?" He said, "Don't worry about it, everything is taken care of." "Now what are your plans?" he asked. I said, "I'm thinking of going home and living with my mother for a while." He gave me money, told me good luck, and told me that whenever I wanted to drive long distance again, I would always have a job. I said, "I can't thank you and the corporation enough." I said, "Where is my helper? I want to thank him for saving my life." The manager said, "He has his own rig now." I said, "That weasel, he finally has the courage to drive on his own." I told him that I had known while he was driving with me that he was a licensed driver. The manager said, "I knew that too, but you were a good team."

HOME AGAIN

I TOOK THE LONG TRAIN ride home. I could not get Daisy off my mind, and I was thinking about my mother. She had no way of knowing where I was or whether I was alive. When I walked in the door that evening my family was having dinner. They all got up to greet me. I said, "I'm just in time, but dinner is on me." I bought food at a Chinese restaurant. We talked until late into the night. They wanted to know why I stayed away for so long and never let them know where I was. I said, "I was driving a truck and was on the road a lot." My mother said, "I heard these stories about truck drivers captured by rebels, tortured and killed. Did you have any of those things happen to you?" I said, "Mom if I did, I would not be here." I told her I had some run-ins, but nothing special. I didn't want my mother to worry.

The next morning, when we were alone, my mother told me that my father told her I did not appreciate what he had done for me, and that I had left without telling him. "He did not tell you the truth," I said. "I was never welcome," I told her. "For the first few weeks I took classes in the evening, but I had to walk for two hours to go to class and back," I said. I told my mother all about my stay. I told her how I always asked for lots of homework. In the morning when his wife's kids were in school, I would do my homework. When her daughters, she had two teenage girls, were home from school they spent a lot of time with me. Then my father told me that doing nothing all day was not good, and I had to find a job. Between work and school, I was doing four hours of walking every day. I told her I could not handle it. His wife called me a wimp and he did nothing about it; that is the reason I left. The man I was working for got me a better job driving trucks, and it worked out well until I got sick. "And now I'm home to stay," I explained.

The house my mother lived in was a small one bedroom. Four people were already living there, but she made room for me. The pension she got from the railroad was not as big as I had thought. I helped my mother as much as I could. My younger brother had a motorcycle, and fancy clothes, but no job. He liked to party and had many friends. He took me to parties and introduced me to his friends, but I did not fit in. He took me for a motorcycle ride; it was a wild ride. My other brother was still in school, Indonesian school. I bought myself a bicycle, but the town was hilly. My mother's sister still lived in the same house, but the young people who used to hang out there had all grown up and moved away. I went to other places I used to hang out but could not find any of my old friends. I went to the truck stops and markets; it was business as usual.

I joined a soccer team. I played but was not into it. One of the soccer players told me that there was a place where they did martial arts: wrestling, boxing and weight

Home Again | 197

training. He said he belonged to the club, and the owner used to be a pro boxer. He told me if I was interested, he would introduce me to the owner. The owner was very friendly. I asked him if I could watch while I was waiting for my friend. He said, "You come and watch anytime." He asked me for my name. He said, "That name is very well known among the Pentjak players." He mentioned some names and asked if I was related to them. I told him I was. "How good are you?" he asked. I said, "I have some training." He said, "When you are ready you are welcome to work out." I went several more times but did not work out. In my mind I could hear Jim telling me to become a familiar face and learn their habits.

The first time I worked out I followed the instructor's commands. He put me with the beginners, and this went on until he thought I had learned enough. The instructor said, "It's sparring time." He turned to me, "Watch really close, so when your turn comes you can defend yourself." In an hour I sparred with all his students. In my mind Jim was telling me that surprise was always best. I was young and eager to show them what I was made of. The instructor wanted to spar with me. I made short work out of him. In the dressing room he said, "I have never had anybody come in and clean our clocks like you did. I have never seen that style of fighting." I told him it was a combination of Pentjak and Judo. The owner called me in the office and offered me a partnership. I said, "What do you want me to do?" He said, "I'm offering you the martial arts department." I said, "I can't accept it, I'm not a Master and I have no rank in Judo."

My mother asked me why I was always home in the evenings. "Why don't you go out, like your brother?" I said, "I want to be with you, I like it this way." My mother said, "Why don't you find yourself a girlfriend?" I said, "I'm not ready." She said, "You are afraid of girls, you've never had a girlfriend." I did not answer and thought if only she knew. My friend asked me why I was not working out at the club anymore. I told him I didn't feel like it. He said, "I saw you spar; I want to learn some of your techniques. I'll pay you for it." I said, "I'll work with you, but I won't take any pay."

My friend introduced me to his family. There were seven kids and the mother: four boys and three girls. The older siblings all had jobs, and the three younger ones were in school. My friend was the only one into martial arts. The other family members played music. It was fun to listen to them make music and sing songs while we were working out in the next room. My friend worked, so we did the workouts in the evening. My mother said, "Finally, you found yourself something interesting enough to go to in the evening." I said, "I made friends with a family, there are seven kids in the family, and they all play music." "When did you get interested in music?" she asked. I said, "I don't play any instruments, I just listen to them play and sing."

One evening, the oldest girl came to my house to go to the movies. While I was getting ready, she talked to my mother. That evening when I got home my mother said, "I'm glad you found a girlfriend." I said, "She is not my girlfriend; she has a boyfriend." "Why is she going out with you?" my mother asked. I said, "I went to the movies with the family." I told her that she was making sure that I would not chicken out. My mother said, "She seems to be a nice girl." I said, "The whole family is nice." Her boyfriend had a good job, but he had to travel. I did not like him.

One evening, I had dinner with the family. Her boyfriend came in drunk, started yelling at her and started to get physical with her in front of everybody. I took him outside and told him to behave. He attacked me, but I worked him over. Then I told him to apologize to his girlfriend and the family, and not to come back unless he was sober. I apologized and told the family that it was better if I stayed away. Her mother said, "You are family, and he needed that."

I told my mother that I went to the Dutch Army motor pool looking for work, but they were not hiring. I met a cousin who worked there, who was still in the military. He took me for a ride in his jeep and told me he would keep in touch. My mother said, "You have another cousin who has a music store; maybe he needs somebody." We went to his house, and my mother introduced me to the family. He said, "This is your long-lost son." My mother said, "Yes, he is looking for work, maybe you could help him?" He hired me and told me to come to the store the next morning.

I went to the store, but he was not there. There were two girls in the store taking care of business. I asked when the boss came in. They said they did not know, and sometimes he didn't come in at all. When the boss came in, he said, "You already met the girls." In the truck he told me that he put in a lot of sound systems for house parties and other get-togethers. He told me I would deliver the stuff. He also installed new appliances. Sometimes the boss needed the truck, so when I had to deliver something from the store, I used his motorcycle.

Sometimes my other cousin came to the store, and he seemed to know one of the girls. I also befriended another man who drove for the military motor pool. I told him that I would buy five gallons of gasoline from him every day. He said, "What makes you think that I have extra gasoline?" "I know, I have worked at the motor pool pumping gasoline," I replied. I told him nobody would find out, and it was safe to sell it to me.

One day, my cousin came to the store and said, "We are going to the resort on the mountain tonight, I have two beauties lined up." I said, "Who is we?" He said, "You and I." I said, "I don't feel like going out with girls." He told me I wouldn't regret going, that they were really nice girls. "Beside that, my jeep has to be push started," he added. We had a lot of fun and a lot of laughs. At work, I was telling the girls how much fun we had. I told them about the jeep that had to be pushed, and that the girl I was sitting next to on the date seemed to like me.

One of the girls at the store said, "The girl you were sitting next to is my sister." I said, "How come I have never seen her before? I go to your house often and visit with your mother when I buy bread from her." She said, "Because she works and lives in Djakarta. She is an airline hostess for the Garuda airlines, but I'll let you know when she is in town." One morning, I was about to go out on my bike when I saw the girl I worked with, her mother and her sister going by my house. I wanted to ignore them, but they were too close, so I turned around to say hi. Her mother invited me to come to their house. I spent the day there, and I did not regret it. It seemed to click between this girl and me. When she was in town, we spent a lot of time together. My mother said, "The girl you spend so much time with is such a lady, I wish you the best." I knew what my mother was saying.

I told my boss that I found another job, driving big rigs. He joked, "I'm getting tired of you anyway." He asked me when I would be starting, and I told him as soon as he let me go. He told me I was free to go. The girls at the store told me to come and visit whenever I was in town. I did, and I continued to help deliver stuff. I worked for a small outfit that specialized in moving households. My rig was a 1941 Chevrolet, with no doors, that had to be crank started. I drove mostly at night and it could be cold in the mountain passes. The part I did not like about driving for a small outfit was that in every town you came in or out of there were policemen checking the papers. However, it was not the papers they were after – it was the money you put in. It was the same thing at the weigh stations. When there was not enough money with the papers, they made you park the truck for an inspection that would take hours. At the truck stop it was not any better. When I stopped to eat or rest, I had to pay for protection, and if I didn't pay, my truck could get sabotaged. With this outfit there was only one motor pool in Djakarta where I could rest and clean up without paying.

    I was tempted to start driving long distance for the corporation I had worked for before. I wouldn't have to mess with the police or other money grabbers. The routes wouldn't go by my hometown though, and at this point I had a girlfriend. There was another trucking outfit close to my work, so I went up there to find out whether they would hire me. The men I talked to said it wasn't easy to get hired by their outfit. They worked many hours without overtime pay. I told them as long as I had been driving trucks, I had never been paid overtime. The pay was not all that good, and they had to load and unload the trucks, but they said they were home every night, and it was only a five-day workweek. This was the job I had been looking for. I went to the office and talked to the owner. He told me if I was willing to work, I could start the next day at seven in the morning. I walked by the men and said, "It was not hard, I'm hired." They asked me what time I would be starting. When I told them 7:00 a.m., they told me I would be loading trucks.

The first day I had to ride with the foreman to the warehouse where they had tea crates ready for export. The boxes were made of thin plywood with metal reinforcements on the outside. At the warehouse we did not load the trucks. The first six trucks were already covered with waterproof tarps ready to leave. We hauled two more loads that had to be unloaded at the motor pool. The foreman did not want me to touch the tea crates. He said there was a special way to unload the boxes. "If you don't throw them flat on top of each other you will puncture a hole in the plywood. Then, the tea is not good for export and the boss will be docked for it, which will come out of your wages," he said. I did not say anything; I just did what I was told. The trucks were ready, but there were no drivers. We finished hauling the tea crates. This job took some getting used to. It was different than driving for the big corporation. I was on my own and did not have to do physical labor.

The foreman said, "Go to the back and let the helpers teach you how to stack tea boxes." It was harder than I expected. Around 5:00 in the afternoon the trucks were coming back to the motor pool empty. I could not understand how they drove all the way to the docks in Djakarta and came back empty. I did not understand how the company could make money this way. The extra three truckloads from the warehouse had to be loaded on the trucks. I did not handle the tea boxes. I was put with the helpers because I had to learn how to put the tarp on and tie it down. In the morning, the trucks were gone. The foreman told me my job was to haul tea from the warehouse to the motor pool. I did not help loading the tea. I spent my free time practicing stacking tea boxes.

One day the foreman said, "You are a good driver; I would like to test you on the route." I asked him to tell me more about the route. He told me he would tell me everything about the route, and if I didn't like it, I wouldn't have to take the route, but the pay was better. He explained that the trucks left the motor pool at 5:00 a.m., and had to be unloaded at the docks in Djakarta before 12:00 p.m. It would take four hours to get to the docks from the motor pool. The trucks went to the truck stop at the zoo in Djakarta because there were no scalpers. By 1:00 p.m. you were on your way back. There were two drivers and a helper on each truck. Any driver who took extra cargo would be fired. The only cargo you could carry back was for the tea plantations that the company had a contract with.

My first trip was with the foreman of the drivers. He was responsible for everything on the road. He was a crazy driver who took too many chances. The first day he did not let me drive. The first time I drove he said that I drove too slow. I always made it in time to the docks and back. We were always the last truck to leave and he got nervous when he didn't see the trucks in front of him. After that I convinced him that it was a good thing that we didn't see the trucks because that meant that everything was in order. I did most of the driving and he slept a lot.

From day one I noticed that two of the trucks hauled extra cargo. I knew it was against the rules, but I was a new driver, so I kept my mouth shut. I didn't know whether the foreman got some of the money. I drove with the foreman, so I could not find out whether the other drivers knew. To my surprise, I found my helper, whom I had been working with on the long haul. I asked him why he was working as a helper. He joked, "In a way I was looking for you. I could ask you the same thing." I said, "You first." He said, "There are no Indonesian drivers at this outfit, and I like to be home at night because I got married." I said, "I'm doing it for the same reason, but I'm not married, I have a girlfriend."

He asked if I ever found out where Nancy lived. He said, "I know where she lives in Djakarta. When you got sick and went home, I took over your route, and I saw her. I wanted to tell her about you, but I didn't because she doesn't know me. She is doing well." I said, "I'm happy for her, but that is behind me." The boss asked the foreman why he didn't let me drive with the other drivers. He told him it was because he liked my driving. It was OK with the other drivers; he drove like a maniac, especially when he was upset about something.

Friday was payday and many times on Monday my foreman would borrow money from me. I asked the other drivers why our foreman was always broke on Mondays. They told me to watch what he did after he got paid. He always went to the bar and got drunk, so drunk that he hardly could walk. I followed him to the bar, and I stayed until it was time for him to go home. Outside the bar he stumbled into one of those bicycle taxis, called a betja. I went with him to make sure that he got home safe. The bicycle taxi driver told me that he had been doing this for some time. The taxi driver always made sure that he got into the house. I said, "How does he pay you?" He said, "I take the money out of his pocket." "All his money?" I asked. He said, "No, sometimes he has no money left,

Home Again | 205

so I go to the motor pool and tell him that he owes me money." I told the taxi driver he was a good person. I tried to get the foreman off the booze, but it did not work.

I asked the foreman if we could change helpers. I told him I would like to work with the helper I had worked with before. "No problem," he said. One morning the foreman told me he had to drop off a package in Djakarta. It was against the rules, but he was driving, so I did not say anything. At the door there was a lady waiting. He gave the package to her, kissed her and came back to the truck. I said, "That is a pretty lady." He said, "That is my girlfriend, we are getting married soon." Every morning he asked if he could stop at his girlfriend's house for five minutes, but he always stayed longer. We were getting pressed for time. I told him I would drop him off at his girlfriend's in the morning and pick him up on the way home. I would take care of the paperwork. He said, "Are you sure you can take care of the paperwork?" I said, "If you think that I could not take care of the paperwork, why don't you drop me off at your girlfriend's house?" He did not say anything but gave me a dirty look. The first time I did the paperwork he checked it. After this, things were running smoothly, and everything was on time.

The other drivers did not like my new set-up. They told me he was using me as his floor mat. I said, "I know it is against the rules, but it is up to you guys to report him." Nobody did. The foreman got married and left the company. The boss called all the drivers to his office and said one of us had to take that job. Nobody volunteered because you got more responsibility, but you were paid the same. Then the boss said, "I have to appoint one of you." One of the drivers suggested the boss should make his partner foreman because he knew how to handle the paperwork.

The boss said to me, "You got the job." I said, "I don't have the seniority to take this job, but if I have to, I want to go over the rules." The boss said the rules will stay the same. I said, "I want you to go over it with all of us: what we can and cannot do." Before we left the room, I said, "We all go by the rules; I will report anybody who doesn't."

The very next morning the two drivers who had always been hauling extra cargo were at it again. I reported them. The boss said, "These two drivers have been with me from the beginning. Have they been doing this all the time?" I told him he would need ask that of the man in charge back then. I was only reporting what I saw now. I told the boss if he didn't do anything about it I would let the other drivers do the same thing. The boss called them to the office. He told them no more extra cargo, but it did not last. I reported them again, and by the third time they got fired. The drivers were very unhappy with me. They told the other drivers that they were going to work me over.

On payday, I saw them waiting for me at the gate but some of the drivers and helpers went with me to confront them. It did not come to a fight. They told me that I did not have a heart and destroyed their living. I said, "I only did what was expected from me." In the meantime, I was taking care of the paperwork and driving by myself, with no extra pay. My helper was a licensed driver, so he helped me with the driving. There were not many Indo drivers who wanted to work for this outfit. We were short on drivers. Everyday there were drivers who had to drive both ways with no extra pay. When they complained to the boss his answer was always, "If you don't like it you can leave."

I asked my helper if he would drive, and I said I could talk to the boss. He said he wanted to stay my helper. I asked the boss if he would hire an Indonesian driver. He

Home Again | 207

said he would rather not. I told him I had worked with this man before, on the long hauls, and he could trust him. If nobody wanted to drive with him, he could be my partner. He got hired, and he was the first non-Indo driver. Now, I had two Indonesians working with me. It was difficult working with an unhappy crew. Many times, I took the wheel from the drivers who had to drive both ways. They told me that that I was favoring the Indonesians. I said, "There are not many Indo drivers left who like to work for this outfit."

In the meantime, I got married. My wife was expecting a baby, so she had to stop working. We were living in the one-car garage at my mother's house. When the baby was born, I did not get a day off. I needed more money and the boss was not about to give us a raise. It was getting to me, working with an unhappy crew for such little money. One day, I told the crew not to leave the truck stop in Djakarta because I wanted a meeting with everybody. I said, "I have a plan, I know you are all unhappy." I told them there was a way to make more money, but we all had to work together. We would load two or three trucks every day and divide the money. "How are we going to divide it?" they asked. I said, "You give the money to me, I'll divide it and you get your share in the morning, but we all have to agree on this." If we got caught, we would all be fired. I told everyone to think about it. One guy said, "How do we know we are getting an equal share?" I said, "You have to trust me, or you can divide the money." The first time we did it I worked it all out on paper and showed it to them at the truck stop. This worked out well for a long time. The helpers always made sure that I got all the money. We were always on time. We did not ask for a raise or more drivers.

Somebody must have told the boss. He set a trap and we were caught. In the office he said, "You know the rules and you were supposed to enforce them, but instead what did you do?" I said, "I know I did wrong and I take full responsibility for it, but I want you to hear my side of the story." He said, "I don't want to hear it. I want you to get off my property and I never want to see you again." I left; at home I said to my wife, "This is the last bundle of money you have to divide, we got caught and I'm fired." She said, "We are expecting our second child, what are you going to do?" I said, "I'll find other work."

At about 5:00 in the morning somebody was knocking on my door. I opened my window and there was my boss shouting at me. I said, "I don't want to hear any of this" and closed the window. He started pounding on my door and I was worried that he would wake up everybody in the house. I went outside and told him to get off my property. He said, "It was not fair for me to tell the drivers not to come to work." I said, "I have nothing to do with that. When you told me to get off the property, I left without talking to any of them." He said, "You know that when the tea doesn't get to the docks in Djakarta, I will lose my contract." I said, "That is not my problem; you fired me." "I'm asking you for help," he pleaded.

I went to a place where I knew that some of the drivers would wait for each other to carpool to work. There were four of them having coffee. I told them that the boss woke me up and said no drivers came to work and that it was my fault. "We all know if the tea doesn't get to the docks in Djakarta, he will lose his contract," they said. "I'm asking you to go to the motor pool and drive today," I said. They told me they would only go if he hired me back. I told them I would go with them to the pool. Only the Indonesian driver showed up. I said to the boss you have eight trucks ready to go, and I got you five drivers that will drive for you today. He said I have six drivers. I said, "You fired me, I'm not driving." He said, "I want you back." I said, "Before I drive for you again, we have to agree on things first." He said, "Name it." I told him I wanted him to double the wages of the drivers and helpers. He told me that would never happen. I told him to think about it and left.

That evening one of the drivers picked me up and told me they we were having a meeting and wanted me there. At the meeting they said the boss offered them more money but made them promise never to take extra cargo. I asked what he offered. They said a 25% raise. I asked if it was for the helpers also. They said the boss did not mention the helpers. I asked how many were willing to take his offer. They said, "It is a lot of money, unless you have a better idea." I said, "I already told the boss that I would drive for him again, only if he doubles our wages including the helpers." They told me that would never happen. I told them that was exactly what he said. I said, "It is a gamble, but think about it." Working for this outfit meant that workers were working without overtime, vacation, health insurance or pension. The boss couldn't find experienced drivers in a day or two and the tea had to be at docks every day. Within a very short time he would lose his contract. I told them to take his offer and come to work in the morning or take the gamble with me and see what happens. They said, "We all have families." I said, "I know, and jobs are hard to find."

At about 8:00 in the morning one of the drivers came to my house and told me the boss wanted to talk to me. The boss told me he wanted to talk in the office. He asked,

"I offered the drivers a 25% raise and you told them not to take it?" I said, "That is not true. I told them to take your offer and go to work, but I would stick to my demand and would not work for you. They are all here, what is the problem?" He said, "They will not drive without you." I said, "Now you have a problem." He said, "I would never give in to your demands." I said, "Well then we have nothing to talk about." That day the drivers went home and told the boss they would not drive without me.

In the meantime, the day crew kept hauling tea from the warehouse for export. In two days, he had so much tea at the motor pool that he had to do something. He came to my house and asked me to talk in his office. At the office, he came up with many different offers. I did not accept. He said, "You win, but I want you to promise me not to haul extra cargo." I said, "The only thing I promise is that the tea gets to the docks on time as long as you keep the trucks in good running condition." The truckers worked hard, no matter how bad it would sometimes get in the rainy season. No complaints and the boss was happy.

One Friday after we got paid, the boss wanted to talk to me in his office. He said he did not get his contract renewed and had only thirty more days on it. He needed me and the crew to deliver the tea until the contract expired. On the last payday the boss had everybody together and told us he had tried to get new contracts, but the Indonesians didn't like to do business with the Dutch anymore. He told us he had his trucking company up for sale. We were out of work.

It was difficult to find a good-paying job. The Indonesians didn't like hiring Indos. We all were Dutch citizens and Holland opened up the country to let us Indos in. Expenses would be covered by the Dutch government.

Most of us didn't know much about Holland other than it was cold in winter. There was a long waiting list at the embassy, my name included. Some of the lucky ones got assistance from the Dutch embassy.

I found work as a day laborer delivering furniture and appliances to the newly rich Indonesians, Chinese and Americans who were in Indonesia as flight instructors for the Indonesian air force. One morning, my helper came over and said, "I got a job for you." I said, "Take me there. I need steady work." My helper introduced me to the young man in the office. He looked at me and said you are not Indonesian. I said, "You are right, I'm not; is there a problem?"

To my surprise, the driver I hired before came in the office and told the young man in charge he would handle this, then told him to leave the office. We talked about the old times when he was driving for me and about the time we were hauling cigarettes. I asked him if he owned the trucking company. He said, "No, but my family does." I asked him why he wanted to hire me. He told me he needed somebody with experience. "These greenhorns don't know much about the trucking business," he said. "And I'm stuck in the office," he added. "What do you want me to do?" I asked. He said, "I'll give you a rig and you make money for me." I said, "You know better, you can't give somebody a truck and expect to make money." I told him we had to put it on paper and figure out what his part of the bargain was and what would be mine. He wrote an amount on paper. I told him I could do that, but I was wondering about the permit. He told me he would take care of the permits. I told my helper this could be easy money.

The companies that were now run by young Indonesians always gave me a hard time. I reported this to the boss and told him about other contracts he could get. I did not feel like begging. I told my helper we could make money if we could get cargo out of rebel territory. I told the boss it was not going to work for me to work with the young Indonesians because they were giving me the runaround. I told him I was willing to get cargo out of rebel country. The boss told me he needed me to get building material from the docks in Djakarta.

I had to haul long pieces of iron and galvanized pipes. There was one intersection where a policeman stood on a podium to direct traffic. I had to make a left turn. We drove on the left side of the road in Indonesia, and because of my long trailer, the traffic never left me enough room to make the turn, but the policemen always took it out on me. Every time I went by there, I would make a traffic jam. The police got so upset with me that one day they made me park the rig and took my driver's license away. We took the bus home. I told the boss what happened. He used to drive for me, so he understood what was going on. He said, "Those policemen are going to be in big trouble." The owner of the corporation was a high-ranking official with the Indonesian government. I asked what he wanted me to do. He told me to go home and wait until I got my driver's license back.

I enjoyed the days off. I was in the house when a policeman on a motorcycle stopped by my house and asked for me. He was very polite and apologetic. He had come to give me my driver's license back. My boss told me go to Djakarta and get the truck back. After this incident whenever I got to the intersection there were three policemen directing traffic, no more problems, and I didn't get stopped at any checkpoints. When my boss wanted to talk to me in his office, he always told the other young men to leave. This time he told me that he got all the contracts I told him about. I said, "Why are you so excited?" He said, "This is a family business and with these contracts you got me I'm top dog; that means a lot to me." I said, "I did not get the contracts for you." He said, "I would never forget who gave me the tip." I said, "Now that you got the contracts and enough drivers you don't need me anymore." He said, "I really want you to run the show." I told him he knew better and that would make him lose the contracts. He told me the first few times he would go to the offices so that they knew who owned the corporation.

Things went smoothly, but I was not happy because I wanted to drive. I asked the boss if he could give me one of his trusted men so I could train him. It took longer than I expected to train him. I told my helper that he should get his own rig and drive for the new contracts. He asked what I was going to do. I told him I was going to drive through rebel country. He said, "There must be a reason for it." I said, "For the money, and I'm tired of being treated like an outsider by these young men in charge." He said, "You know better than anybody, when you go out there, that will put you in danger." I told him that was why I wanted him to have his own rig so he could be home with his family. I told him I would drive through rebel country by myself so that I wouldn't put anybody else in danger. He said, "I go where you go, you're my brother." I replied, "Have it your way."

I went to the Dutch embassy to check if I could go to Holland on their cost. They had a long waiting list. At home, I told my wife to check how much it would cost to go on our own. She said, "It is about time, when you are not home somebody has rattled the door. I don't know if they are trying to scare me or hurt me." I went to the night watchman across the street. He was keeping an eye on the property of the American pilots. I asked him to keep an eye on my house. He said, "I could do that." I gave him money.

The boss gave me the newest truck. I don't know why this man went all out to help me. All my business was with the Chinese. When I drove to rebel country, I always wore the headband Victor gave me. I was hauling firewood, wood coal, produce, and fruit. One day, I had a load of citrus fruit when my truck broke down in a town just outside of rebel country. I remembered that the girl I worked with at the music store married an Indonesian and moved to this town. I did not know her married name. I knew that her husband was the prison warden in town. I asked somebody on the street if he knew where the warden lived. He told me he would take me there.

I knocked on the door. She looked at me and told me to come in. She said, "I never expected to see you again, you're still driving trucks?" I said, "Yes, and I'm in trouble. I have a load of citrus fruit, Djeroek Garoet, and if I don't make it to the big city in two days, I'll lose a lot of money." She asked if I drove through rebel country. I said, "Yes, that is all I do. A trucker like me can't make a living in the big city." She told me the week before there was some shooting at the edge of town between the rebels and the military. I said, "Let's forget about the rebels." "How long has it been since we have seen each other?" I asked. She said, "About seven years, I miss my friends from the big city." She said, "How about you, are you married?" I told her I was. She said, "You must have a death wish driving through rebel country." I said, "No, I have to do what I have to, to support my family."

She called her husband. She was a fortunate person in this time to have a telephone. Her husband was a nice person. He said, "My wife has told me a lot about you." I said, "We worked at the music store and we are friends." He asked where my truck was. I said, "Parked at the edge of town; my helper stayed with the truck." He said, "I'll send a mechanic and if he can't repair it the truck will be towed to the shop." She said, "Do you still have the same helper, your slave?" "Yes, we get along fine, and he doesn't trust me by myself," I joked. We talked for hours, then she told her husband to check on the truck and invite my helper to the house. Her husband said the truck was in the shop, and the mechanic found the problem, but he couldn't repair it because the truck needed a new part. I asked what it was. He told me it was the fuel pump. I asked if there was a part store in this town. He said, "Yes, the mechanic already checked, and they don't have one that will fit your truck." I figured it would take four days for the fuel pump to come from the big city. I told him I might as well dump my load at the local market and hope to get my money back. He said, "I don't think so." I said, "Then I'll donate it to the prison."

He said, "Forget about the truck, for now let's go to dinner in town, and we'll show you the town." I told them I had no good clothes to go to town. Instead I would go to the market with my helper, have something to eat, and find a place to sleep. She said, "You both are staying here tonight, and you are the same size as my husband; let's find out if I can dress you." His clothes fit me, even his shoes. I felt uncomfortable in a suit and tie. My helper did not go with us. They took me to an upscale restaurant. Everybody in town knew my friend and her husband. We went to different places in town, and whenever she saw friends, she introduced me as her brother.

The next day was Saturday, and my cargo was taken to the prison. I asked the warden what the best way was to order a new fuel pump. He said, "I can order it for you, but the order would not go out until Monday and if I ordered it from the part store it might take longer." They wouldn't order just one item from a part store. I was trying to find a way to let my boss know what the problem was. The warden said, "My wife has lunch ready and is waiting for us." During lunch I told them it would take four days before I could get on the road again. I needed to find a way to let my boss know that I was okay. The warden said he could send a telegram. I also needed to find a place to stay. She said, "You'll stay here, we have a lot to talk about."

Back at the prison, the warden was ready to send a telegram when the mechanic came in and told him that a truck on the property had a fuel pump that would fit my truck. The warden told him to take it off and put it on my truck. I said, "I appreciate what you are doing for me, and I will pay whatever it costs." The warden said, "It will cost you nothing. I'll send the old fuel pump to the office in the city and they'll send me a new one." I said, "What about the mechanic?" The warden said, "That is his job." That evening I said, "I'd like to leave early, so that I can find some cargo to take to the city. I can't thank you enough for what you did for me." My friend said, "You're not leaving until after breakfast." I said, "I would like to be out of rebel country before dark." The warden said, "If you don't mind, I have some cargo that has to go to the city." His wife said, "Do it for me." I told them this was wonderful. The warden said, "You stay at the house, keep

Home Again | 217

my wife company, and my men will load the truck." My helper said he would go with the warden.

My friend said, "Let's go to the market and buy some stuff for lunch and dinner." I said, "I'd like to leave after lunch." She said you're not leaving until tomorrow. She told one of her servants to come with us. She bought a lot of stuff at the market and this poor woman had to carry everything. I didn't leave until late afternoon the next day. I told the warden before I left that I wanted to thank the mechanic. I thanked him and gave him money.

On the way home my helper said, "You always get out of bad situations." I said, "So far we got lucky, it is your turn to drive." I told the boss what happened and told him to have somebody deliver this stuff because he might get some business out of it. I wanted to take some time off. My boss said, "That gives us time to work on your truck." From then on when I went in the direction of my friends, I would visit them. I parked my truck at the prison motor pool and the mechanic would always check the truck.

One day the Chinese businessman I was hauling firewood for told me that there was a kind of wood deep in rebel territory that he would like to have. I asked how I could get it. He told me you had to be introduced by somebody, but your safety was not guaranteed. "I'll pay you extra good," he said. "That doesn't do me any good if they kill me," I replied. He told me to think about it. I told my helper about the deal. He said, "You must have a death wish, those people will kill you without asking any questions." I said, "That is why I told you this, I don't want you to go with me." My boss wanted me to haul cargo from the motor pool to Djakarta and bring cargo back from the docks in Djakarta. This was a safe route. I drove at night and my helper drove us back during the day. I thought that it was only one trip, but it took much longer.

One evening, on my way to Djakarta, I met my brother-in-law. He drove for another trucking company. He said, "We are going the same direction, I'll follow you." I said, "I drive straight through until the last truck stop before Djakarta." We got to the truck stop late at night. It was deserted; even the kampong village behind the truck stop was empty. We ate, then went to sleep. The next morning, we freshened up and my brother-in-law started to make coffee. An older lady, the owner, showed up and asked us how we got through. I asked her what she meant, because everything was quiet last night; there wasn't even a dog on the road. She told us there was a battle all day and night between the army and the rebels. I told her we must have gotten through after it was over.

I was hauling firewood again when the Chinese businessman told me that there was a man who could introduce me to the rebels in the mountains. I told him I was not interested. I was driving through rebel country every day. It had become routine for me. I already went to places where Indonesian drivers did not go. The thought of going into the mountains and making so much more money stuck in my head. One day I said to my helper, "It is time you get your own rig; I have decided to go to the mountains and haul lumber." He said, "You're crazy and you are pushing your luck." I said, "We go through rebel country all the time." He said, "We got to know those people, they work with us."

I was delivering firewood and told the Chinese man that I would go to the mountains and get him the lumber he wanted. He said, "I'll let you know when your contact man is here." My helper said, "This time you're pushing it, and I'm not going with you." I said, "Tomorrow we'll go talk to the boss, so you can get your own rig, but I don't want you to tell him where I'm going." At home I never told my family where I was going. I only told them that some of the trips took longer. As far as they knew I was only driving where it was safe.

The day came that I was going to get lumber. My helper told me if he wanted his own truck, he would talk to the boss himself. I said, "Have it your way, I have to get my truck ready." He said, "That is my job." The next day it was time to meet the contact person. I got to the motor pool and my helper was sitting in the truck. I asked him what he was doing. He said, "I'm going where you go." My contact person was an older man, a very nice person. He told me everything that was going on at the mountains. He said, "When you get accepted, these people will take care of you." I said, "Why is it so hard to work with these people?" He said, "They are afraid that somebody is pretending to buy lumber and is a spy for the government." He told me it took two days to get to the sawmill, one day to load, and two days to drive back.

I asked the Chinese man how much it was worth to him. He told me to bring him the lumber and we would figure it out. I said, "I want to know how much it is worth to you for me to risk my life." He gave me money, a lot of money, and said "This is for you to pay for the wood and expenses." I said, "That's a good start." My contact man told me to stop at a truck stop deep in rebel country. I asked if there would be trucks coming through. He told me many trucks came through during the day. I did not see any. The contact man spoke to the woman who ran the place. Then he told me to park the truck and come with him. He told my helper to stay with the truck.

We walked through the kampong to a house and he told me to wait while he got the man I needed to meet. I waited for a long time; a woman gave me something to eat and some tea. The men came back and the contact man said, "This is the man you'll do business with." He looked at my headband but did not say anything. He was a good-looking young man. He said, "You want to do business with us?" I said, "Only if you want me to." He said, "Tonight somebody will drive you to the sawmill, your helper will stay at the truck stop." Late at night, two men came to the truck stop, blindfolded me and took off. I did not know what direction we were going. At the sawmill, they took my blindfold off. I could see the sun was already coming up and it was cold high up in the mountains.

At the sawmill they rolled the logs onto scaffolds. There was a man standing on top and one on the ground pulling on a long saw blade to make the lumber. They loaded the truck the same way, piece by piece, all manpower. The man I met at the house told me he would take me back to the truck stop and pay me there. He blindfolded me again. When we got to the truck stop the sun was going down. I asked the man, "How much do I owe you?" He took me to a room and wrote the amount on a piece of paper. It was very reasonable. I said, "I'll get the money; my helper has it on him." I said to the man, "I would like to come back and do business with you again." He said, "How long does it take you to come back?" I told him about five days. He told me he would be waiting for me.

The woman at the truck stop took good care of us. The next morning before we left, I asked the woman if she needed anything from the city. She said, "Money is scarce here, I don't need anything, but if you could bring a barrel of kerosene that would help the mountain people a lot." When I drove up to the lumberyard the Chinese man was all smiles, and he said, "You did come back with the wood I want." "What did you expect?" I asked. He said, "I tried before. That driver did not come back." I thought to myself, "You son of a bitch, you never told me this!" I went to the office and gave my boss money. He said, "Why so much?" I said, "I want you to have my truck in the best possible condition because where I'm going a breakdown means trouble and I won't be able to contact you." I gave him two days to work on the truck.

From then on all I did was haul lumber. Every trip went easier. I had them make a list of what they needed from the city. I would not charge them for transportation and in turn they gave me a discount on the lumber. They made it so easy for me. I didn't have to go to the sawmill anymore; I stayed at the truck stop. The woman and her daughters at the truck stop became my good friends. The woman told me that her daughters had a Dutch father, but he never claimed them, so they grew up in the kampong. Then she told me the man I was doing business with had a Dutch father too. She explained this happened a lot when the plantations were run by the Dutch. She only told me to stay out of sight on Fridays when they were praying. I tried not to be there on Fridays.

One night on my way home the generator on the truck went out. I only drove by the people I did business with at night time. By daylight, somebody I never saw before came to me and asked if I knew what the problem was. I said, "the generator, I need a new one." He told me to take it off because he was going to the city and could get me a new one. Not long after that, another man stopped and said, "I'll take you back to the truck stop." I said, "What about my truck?" He said, "We'll make sure nothing will happen to it. In the meantime, they charged my truck battery. At the truck stop, I asked the woman who the men were that helped me. She said, "They are all part of the organization; you can trust them." I did not know that I was not a stranger to these people.

I asked the woman at the truck stop how long it would take before I could get the new part for the truck. She told me two to four days. I said, "Is there something we could help you with at the store?" She said, "This is a good time to get to know us better." The girls showed me and my helper the plantations and we visited with many people in the kampong. A man came and told us the truck was ready to go. I asked the woman how much I owed. She told me she didn't charge her guests. I gave her money and told her to buy something for the girls. The generator was already in place. I paid the man and went on my way. I told my helper to drive. I was thinking about this beautiful country and the people I loved. I had made up my mind to leave the country and it made me so sad.

I knew what I was doing: I could not go on, and I could not live in the city and raise my family. I was crying quietly. My helper said, "What is wrong with you, are you having a malaria attack?" I said, "There is nothing wrong with me, keep on driving. I told my wife we had enough money to leave Indonesia, and she could find booking to go to Holland. About two months later my wife told me she had booked us on an Italian ship and that we only had a few weeks to get the papers in order."

I told my boss that I was leaving the country and would not drive for him anymore. He could not believe what I was saying. He said, "You are doing so well, you were born in this country, and now you want to go to a country you don't know? Tell me what is troubling you,

Home Again | 223

and let me help." I said, "It is not safe here, when I'm on the road people have tried to break into my house. I don't know if they're trying to scare my wife or want to hurt her." What I was doing could not last forever. I told him if the rebels thought that I was a spy they would kill me, and if the police or the military knew what I was doing they would lock me up. He said, "I don't think that the rebels would ever hurt you." I said, "How do you know?" He said, "Nobody has ever gotten away with what you are doing. If the rebels thought that you were a spy, they would have killed you a long time ago." Then he added, "The housing problem I can help you with. I'll build you a house on my property where nobody can bother you. So that you're not driving through dangerous country or not driving at all, I'll get you a job in the office here with me," he said. With tears in my eyes, I asked, "Why are doing all this for me?" He said, "I consider you my son and I want you to have the best."

We sat in silence, then I got up and said, "I have decided to leave the country and take my family to a foreign place." He said, "I can't stop you and I respect your decision." We shook hands and we both had tears in our eyes. I left his office a broken man. Outside, my helper said, "Why are you crying so much these days?" I said, "I'm leaving Indonesia, I'm going to the Netherlands." He said, "You are not leaving, this is your country, you were born here." I said, "Don't make it more difficult than it already is."

The next morning, my helper was sitting on my front porch. I asked him what he was doing. He said, "Waiting for you to go to work." I told him I was not going to work, and that I was leaving the country. He would not take no for an answer. This lasted five days. I told my helper I couldn't take him to Holland with me. He said, "I don't want to go to Holland, I want you to go to work with me and stay in Indonesia." I said, "Here is my headband; wear it when you drive through rebel country." In March of 1955 I left Indonesia and took my wife and my two little girls on an Italian ship to the unknown.

WHAT IS AN INDO?

WHEN THE SPANIARDS CAME to Mexico and married Mexican women, their children were Mexicans. The same with the Portuguese in Brazil: their offspring were Brazilians and the same with the English in India. This was not the case with the Dutch in Indonesia. When they married Indonesians, their children, the Indo, were considered Dutch.

When Indonesia won independence from the Netherlands, the Indo became foreigners in their own country.

ABOUT THE AUTHOR

RENÉ LEIDELMEYER WAS BORN in Indonesia in March 1930. He escaped the fatality of war, and immigrated to Holland with his wife and two daughters in 1955. He later expanded his family and immigrated to the United States in 1961.

His family spent two years in California and then moved to Oregon, where René worked as the head groundskeeper for the Primate Research Center for twenty-nine years. In 1967, Sensei René started the judo club called Ojukan. He is a member of the US Judo Federation, and earned a 6th degree black belt.

René retired from the Primate Research Center in the 1990s to dedicate his time to his family, and to his many passions, including bowling, which he still enjoys. René is living happily alongside his wife of sixty-six years, and is surrounded by his five children, eleven grandchildren, and his thirteen great-grandchildren. René is so happy to debut his very first published book.

CPSIA information can be obtained
at www.ICGtesting.com
Printed in the USA
JSHW020143140920
7741JS00003B/13

9 781629 016689